Praise for

BE
FEARLESS

"An inspiring book by an inspiring leader. Jean Case has been in the arena as a technology pioneer and philanthropist, and this book is full of stories and advice to embolden you to take bolder risks and have bigger impact."

—Adam Grant, #1 *New York Times* bestselling author
of *Originals*, *Give and Take*,
and *Option B* with Sheryl Sandberg

"If you want to get back on track, it is time to get fearless."

—Soledad O'Brien interviewing Jean Case on
Matter of Fact with Soledad O'Brien

"Through compelling storytelling, Jean Case shows how bold decision-making and acts of fearlessness have transformed the world. *Be Fearless* stresses one of the most critical components of successful entrepreneurship: discomfort. Her very useful roadmap shows budding entrepreneurs how to think independently and move beyond their comfort zone. Starting a business is not easy, but *Be Fearless* gives entrepreneurs the tools they need to embark— fearlessly—on their own journey."

—Tory Burch, designer and CEO, Tory Burch LLC

"Jean Case has spent years traveling and meeting Americans from many backgrounds and writes about her formula for overcoming doubts and achieving one's dream."

—Judy Woodruff interviewing Jean Case on
PBS NewsHour

"Just reading the contents page is inspiring . . . yes this is good!"

—Norah O'Donnell interviewing Jean Case on
CBS This Morning

"Jean Case has done what many before her have tried but been unable to achieve: break down the essential qualities and principles that drive success. Her book tells us in no uncertain terms what it takes to break through in an increasingly crowded world of ideas. With legitimately surprising research and compelling stories, *Be Fearless* inspires us all to take risks we usually wouldn't, conquer the fears that get in our way, and lead a fulfilling life of clear purpose and maximum impact."

—Eric Schmidt, former executive chairman,
Google and Alphabet Inc.

"I wish I had Jean Case's *Be Fearless* by my side when we were starting Warby Parker. This engaging book highlights stories of ordinary people who end up doing extraordinary things, much to the surprise of others and even themselves, and draws out the 'secret sauce' behind success. For anyone looking to make a change, start a company, or change the world, *Be Fearless* provides both the inspiration and tools to make a real impact."

—Neil Blumenthal, cofounder and co-CEO,
Warby Parker

"*Be Fearless* is part business how-to, part cheerleader on how to get stuff done. If you're stuck, need inspiration, or some ideas on how to move any part of an idea or enterprise forward, it's filled with stories from real people doing incredibly difficult things—from philanthropy to enterprise—and Case's own tough-love advice on making progress."
—GeekWire

"The stories in this book will inspire and motivate you to be brave and bold in unconventional ways. Jean Case creates a narrative of testimonies that can guide you through any challenge or road-block. Confronting the status quo can intimidate many, however *Be Fearless* provides antidotes from thought leaders, entrepreneurs, and everyday people who have defied all odds."
—Mellody Hobson, president,
Ariel Investments

"In need of an inspirational call to action? Jean Case, the first female Chairman of the National Geographic Society, sets out to show how five principles can change your life. She traces how innovators and icons—from Jane Goodall to José Andrés—have succeeded by placing a big bet, taking bold risks, learning from their failures, reaching beyond their bubbles, and allowing urgency to conquer fear."
—*Town & Country Magazine*

"When the going gets tough, crack open *Be Fearless* for a jolt of examples of how entrepreneurs and leaders have broken through and to be inspired to keep pushing forward on your own journey to change the world."
—Brad Feld, entrepreneur and venture capitalist
at Foundry Group

"She offers five principles to help Americans during these divided times that we are currently facing."

—Stephanie Ruhle interviewing Jean Case
on MSNBC

"If you feel stuck in your career, Case's principles are the answer! . . . The book is packed with inspiring examples of success stories."

—*Focus Magazine*

"Case's new book profiles leaders who have used their desire to solve a problem to drown out their fear of risk or failure."

—*Fast Company*

BE FEARLESS

**5 PRINCIPLES FOR A LIFE OF
BREAKTHROUGHS AND PURPOSE**

JEAN CASE

FOREWORD BY JANE GOODALL

Simon & Schuster Paperbacks

New York   London   Toronto   Sydney   New Delhi

Simon & Schuster Paperbacks
An Imprint of Simon & Schuster, Inc.
1230 Avenue of the Americas
New York, NY 10020

First Simon & Schuster paperback edition January 2020

SIMON & SCHUSTER PAPERBACKS and colophon are registered trademarks of Simon & Schuster, Inc.

For information about special discounts for bulk purchases, please contact Simon & Schuster Special Sales at 1-866-506-1949 or business@simonandschuster.com.

The Simon & Schuster Speakers Bureau can bring authors to your live event. For more information or to book an event, contact the Simon & Schuster Speakers Bureau at 1-866-248-3049 or visit our website at www.simonspeakers.com.

Interior design by Carly Loman

Manufactured in the United States of America

10 9 8 7 6 5 4 3 2 1

Library of Congress Cataloging-in-Publication Data
Names: Case, Jean, author.
Title: Be fearless : 5 principles for a life of breakthroughs and purpose / Jean Case.
Description: New York : Simon & Schuster, [2019] | Includes bibliographical references and index.
Identifiers: LCCN 2018034852 (print) | LCCN 2018037028 (ebook) | ISBN 9781501196362 (ebook) | ISBN 9781501196348 (hardcover : alk. paper)
Subjects: LCSH: Courage. | Change (Psychology) | Organizational change. | Social change. | Conduct of life.
Classification: LCC BJ1533.C8 (ebook) | LCC BJ1533.C8 C37 2019 (print) | DDC 155.2/4—dc23

ISBN 978-1-5011-9634-8
ISBN 978-1-5011-9635-5 (pbk)
ISBN 978-1-5011-9636-2 (ebook)

To each person who has heard that voice whisper,
"This is your moment"—
and is choosing to heed the call.

And to all of those who have inspired and supported
my own fearless journey.

Dear Gaston,
Welcome in the SC
world of Schindler.
Looking forward to
rock with you the SC
Quality to the top level
within our industry in US.
But beside the hard work I'm
sure, we will have a lot of
fun. :) Regards

If you added up all the times you failed,
all the times you came up short,
would you try again?

What if failure wasn't a limitation?
What if taking risks was your status quo?
What kind of world would you imagine?

When the challenges we face seem overwhelming,
we need to experiment with new thinking and try new things,
create unlikely partnerships
and set audacious goals.

To build a better world,
to make a real difference,
we have to take bigger risks,
make bigger bets.
And if we fail and fail again,
we have to get right back up and dream even bigger.

To live in a world worth living in,
we have to let challenge inspire us.
We have to take risks, be bold, and fail forward.
We have to *Be Fearless*.

CONTENTS

PART FOUR: REACH BEYOND YOUR BUBBLE

PART FIVE: LET URGENCY CONQUER FEAR

FOREWORD

BY JANE GOODALL

One of the most important messages that I share with people as I travel around the world is that each one of us has some role to play, each one of us makes some impact on the environment, on our community, every day. And we can choose what sort of difference we want to make.

As you read National Geographic Society Chairman Jean Case's *Be Fearless: 5 Principles for a Life of Breakthroughs and Purpose,* you'll see this is one of the key messages to her readers. This message resonates throughout her call for each of us to be fearless—or rather that we must, when necessary, overcome our fear to do what we know is right.

I know the importance of these messages, as the call to Be Fearless has been at the center of my entire life. I was fortunate. By the time I was ten years old, I knew I wanted to go to Africa to live with wild animals and write books about them. Fortunately, I had a wonderful and supportive mother. When everyone else told me to dream about something I could actually achieve—after all, we had very little money, World War II was raging, Africa seemed very far away, and I was a mere *girl*—my mother simply told me I would have to work very hard, take advantage of all opportunities—and never give up. I wish she was alive now so she could know how many people have said to me, "Thank you, Jane. You taught me that because you could do it, I can do it too."

Well, it is well-known that I did get to Africa and that I had the amazing opportunity to live and learn from the animals most like us, the chimpanzees. No one had done this before. People often ask me, "Weren't you afraid when you were out there alone in the forest?" Of course I was sometimes. We are meant to be, as fear gets the adrenaline flowing through our veins and gives us the courage to do what seems impossible. I was afraid when I heard the strange growling, roaring call of a leopard at night when I was sleeping alone under the stars to be close to the chimps when they woke in the morning. I told myself it would be okay—and pulled the blanket over my head! I was afraid when two bull buffalo charged out of the undergrowth—it was the surge of adrenaline that enabled me to climb a seemingly unclimbable tree. (It took more courage to, eventually, climb down, not knowing if they were still hiding, waiting for me. Luckily, they were not!) I was afraid when a group of chimps, having lost their fear of me, treated me like a predator, screaming, shaking branches, and charging. I acted as though I had no interest in them, dug a little hole in the ground, pretended to eat leaves—and eventually they went away!

Finally, all the chimps got used to me, so I could move right up to them. I soon recognized them as individuals, gave them names, got to know their very different personalities. And I learned that their communication gestures—kissing, embracing, patting one another, begging with outstretched hand, and so on—were almost the same as ours and used in the same context. I watched them use grass stems to fish for termites. I noted that their emotions, too, were similar to (or maybe the same as) ours in terms of happiness, sadness, fear, anger, depression, and grief.

It was a magical time in my life.

Then, after I had been with the chimps just over a year, I had to go to Cambridge University to work for a PhD in animal behavior—even though I had never been to college. There I had to Be Fearless and overcome a very different kind of fear: imagine how I felt when professors, of whom I was in awe, told me I had done everything wrong. I should not have given the chimpanzees names—numbers would have been more scientific. I should not talk about their personalities, minds, or emotions—those were qualities unique to humans. Fortunately, as I had not been to college, no one had told me this! Moreover, I had a wonderful childhood teacher—my dog, Rusty! You cannot share your life in a meaningful way with *any* animal and not know that we are *not* the only beings with minds, personalities, and, above all, emotions. My mother always told me that if I believed I was right, I must have the courage of my convictions. So it was Rusty and my mother who helped me overcome my fear and stand up to those professors.

Today Mother Nature needs our help. Chimpanzees, who have taught us so much, are in desperate trouble—along with so many other wonderful animals and plants—as their forests are disappearing. It is the same with woodlands, wetlands, savannas, and virtually all habitats. We are losing biodiversity. We are polluting land, rivers, and oceans. Human populations and our planet are plagued by numerous challenges, with a great need to find sustainable solutions for the future.

And that is why this book is so timely. There is no point in history when it has been more important to Be Fearless, overcome our acceptance of the status quo, and for each of us to step up and take action to make a difference in our world.

We must work to empower everyone to take action to improve bad situations, right perceived wrongs. And *Be Fearless* brings together the tools and stories that can inspire and empower everyone to take exactly that kind of action.

I see the value of this message every day through the work of Roots & Shoots, the Jane Goodall Institute's environmental and humanitarian movement for young people around the world, from kindergarten through higher education, that I started in 1991. Today there are more than 100,000 active Roots & Shoots groups in seventy countries, comprised of young people working to improve things for people, animals, and the environment. The most important message of Roots & Shoots is that every single individual makes a difference every day. And in some cases this means overcoming fear. We must not be afraid to stand up for what we believe in, to make the right choices. And when millions and millions of people make ethical choices, this will, cumulatively, move us toward a better world.

So now, as you read Jean Case's book, *Be Fearless*, I hope that if you are not already engaged in some activity, you will hear the call to action and know that you, too, can change the world. The stories Jean has brought together in this book to bring the Be Fearless principles to life prove that everyone can make a difference. It does not have to be earth-shattering. Try volunteering to help organizations that are working in areas that you feel are important—like clearing trash, visiting old people abandoned by their families, or working in animal shelters for homeless dogs or cats. Get active in campaigns to protect an environment under threat from development, or from fracking. Try to learn more about what is going on—around you, or in the wider world. Sooner or later, you will discover the issue that truly rouses your passion, makes you sad, indignant, angry. And then, roll up your sleeves, take action, and BE FEARLESS.

Jane Goodall, PhD, DBE

Founder, the Jane Goodall Institute,
and United Nations Messenger of Peace

www.janegoodall.org

INTRODUCTION

FINDING FEARLESS

This book is a call to action for those who seek to live extraordinary lives. Maybe that's you.

If you think that only a rare genius, an exceptionally privileged individual, or a massively funded organization can launch a breakthrough product or bring a world-changing movement to life, I'll introduce you in these pages to the fearless people from all walks of life who have made the unimaginable possible. You might be dazzled by their achievements, and it's easy to assume they possessed extraordinary abilities or advantages that set them apart from ordinary strivers. But I have news for you. Their single common trait was this: they were all passionate about making the world better. They seized an opportunity and kept at it in spite of daunting barriers, frequent failures, and loud objections—and they succeeded. Today we look at them, our most iconic creators, and wonder how the world ever existed without their contributions. But, as you will see here, many of their stories provide inspiration and helpful hints on how we can all make a greater impact in every aspect of our lives, and serve as beacons of fearlessness for others.

Today's global challenges—poverty, civil unrest, political stale-mates, economic divisions, climate change—play out daily against the backdrop of our living rooms. But if these problems seem too big and complex—easier to ignore than to even attempt to solve—know that there has never been a better time to engage. An explosion of technological innovation is transforming the way we live. And if we're going to keep up with the rapid pace of change, we need to rethink the old ways of doing things.

My husband, Steve, and I started the Case Foundation in 1997 with a fearless mission: *to invest in people and ideas that can change the world*. This means we're always investigating and experimenting to find the best ideas out there, the best leaders, the best models for innovation. A few years ago, we engaged a team of experts to deter-mine the "secret sauce" that propelled those rare leaders, organiza-tions, and movements to success. They discovered five principles that are consistently present when transformational breakthroughs take place. To spark this sort of change, you must:

1. **Make a Big Bet.** So many people and organizations are naturally cautious. They look at what seemed to work in the past and try to do more of it, leading to only incre-mental advances. Every truly history-making transforma-tion has occurred when people have decided to go for revolutionary change.

2. **Be bold, take risks.** Have the guts to try new, unproven things and the rigor to continue experimenting. Risk tak-ing is not a blind leap off a cliff but a lengthy process of trial and error. And it doesn't end with the launch of a product or the start of a movement. You need to be will-

ing to risk the *next* big idea, even if it means upsetting your own status quo.

3. **Make failure matter.** Great achievers view failure as a necessary part of advancing toward success. No one seeks it out, but if you're trying new things, the outcome is by definition uncertain. When failure happens, great innovators make the setback matter, applying the lessons learned and sharing them with others.

4. **Reach beyond your bubble.** Our society is in thrall to the myth of the lone genius. But innovation happens at intersections. Often the most original solutions come from engaging with people with diverse experiences to forge new and unexpected partnerships.

5. **Let urgency conquer fear.** Don't overthink and overanalyze. It's natural to want to study a problem from all angles, but getting caught up in questions like "What if we're wrong?" and "What if there is a better way?" can leave you paralyzed with fear. Allow the compelling need to act to outweigh all doubts and setbacks.

These five principles can be summarized in two words: Be Fearless. Taken together, they form a road map for effective change-making for people from all walks of life, but it's important to note that they aren't "rules." They don't always work in tandem or sequentially, and none is more important than another. Think of them as a set of markers that can help identify when decisions are being made fearlessly.

We knew we were onto something when we shared these principles with friends and colleagues and started hearing from people in the private, public, nonprofit, and philanthropic sectors who wanted to incorporate the principles into their own work.

Whenever I speak about being fearless, audiences are excited by how tangible the principles are. As someone said to me, "These are things I can do!" People often come up afterward and tell me their own stories of fearlessness, which light up my imagination and fill me with awe: a fourteen-year-old girl who created a nonprofit to cleanly dispose of prescription pills and drugs; a man who started a bakery to employ "unemployable" men and women just released from prison; a Cuban immigrant who created a formula for afford-able assisted living; a Liberian activist who designed a program to help remote communities access medical clinics; a young farmer who invented a no-till process that will save one of earth's most precious resources; a celebrity chef from Washington, DC, who figured out how to serve millions of meals to hurricane victims in dire straits.

These people dreamed big, but most of them started with small, familiar steps. Reading their stories is like following a trail of bread crumbs: They made phone calls. They knocked on doors. They wrote their visions in big letters. They talked and talked and walked and walked. They found supportive communities. They didn't take no for an answer. They did things anyone can do.

Whether you're working at a start-up, finding yourself at a per-sonal crossroads, working as part of an established organization, or looking for inspiration to make a life-altering change, the Be Fear-less principles can provide guidance on how to take that next step. And the moment to do so is now.

I am always inspired by people who challenge themselves and those around them by asking the question: "What would you do if you weren't afraid?" *Be Fearless* tells the stories of innovators and activists, artists and entrepreneurs, scientists and explorers, and individuals from organizations and businesses who answered that question with actions that spoke louder than words. Some of these individuals are household names; others you might never have heard of. As you read about them, I hope you'll imagine yourself standing in their company.

MY STORY

LEAVING NORMAL BEHIND

My personal journey to becoming fearless began in the most normal way—literally. I grew up in the small town of Normal, Illinois, smack-dab in the middle of the American heartland. Normal in the 1960s was the home of Illinois State University, State Farm Insurance, and the first Steak 'n Shake restaurant in the country, whose tagline—"In sight, it must be right"—was an ode to the virtue of transparency. Customers marveled to see delicious burgers prepared right before their eyes.

Like a lot of towns in the Midwest, Normal had a mix of blue-collar workers, small-business owners, educators, business executives, and people who struggled to make it from paycheck to paycheck. The houses on the lane where my family lived belonged to professors from Illinois State University, the owner of the town's A&W drive-in franchise, factory workers, and long-haul truckers like my dad.

Normal was the kind of place where everyone knew your name. My backyard was a cornfield, and I would race through the narrow rows that separated the stalks, exploring the surrounding fields and streams. I was sometimes mistaken for a boy with my cropped hair and sweatshirts—and when I wasn't roaming, I could be found playing pickup sports with the boys in the neighborhood. When I'd take a turn as quarterback, my older brothers would be on the front line, taking on anyone trying to get to me. (Although they'd later tell me, "If you want a boy to like you, you should let him win when you go one-on-one with him in basketball.")

Mom and Dad had moved the family to Normal from Chicago, thinking that this smaller community would be a better environment for raising kids. And while things were good in those early years, as we grew Mom became increasingly concerned that the town offered limited paths of opportunity. She had big dreams for her children and worried we'd get stuck if we stayed.

At about the same time Mom was beginning to worry about our future, my first life-altering experience took place: my parents divorced. That left Mom a single mother of four working as a waitress at night to make ends meet. Those were times of struggle, but fortunately, my mother's parents were there to help.

My grandparents had come to America from Germany on the eve of the Great Depression. Not speaking English, they'd set out to find whatever work they could. For my grandfather, this meant hauling pianos to upstairs apartments in buildings without elevators. My grandmother made beer in her bathtub to sell to the other German immigrants in the neighborhood. (These were Prohibition years.) As their English improved, so did their prospects for work. Within their first decade in America they became small-business owners, beginning with a curtain cleaning business in Chicago before they eventually settled in Normal's twin city, Bloomington, where they bought and ran a hotel near Main Street.

It was in that hotel that I got my first sense of business life.

Mom's night shift as a waitress left her days free, so she'd routinely bundle us up and we'd head to the hotel to help in whatever way we could. My brothers shoveled coal into the furnace, and my sister and I ran errands or did chores. I felt like I was the luckiest kid alive when I got to sit behind the large reception desk and pretend I was in charge. There was a large glass case with candy and some essentials, and my grandmother noticed that guests were much more inclined to buy something if I was behind the counter. She figured everyone was trying to be nice to "the kid," so she encouraged me to greet guests or hang out next to her as she worked behind the counter.

My grandparents' fearless American journey and their tireless work ethic provided an early lesson for me that one could start out without many resources, connections, or skills—including language—and build lives of consequence. In addition to their contribution to our lives, they were civic leaders in our town and were widely respected for their many contributions.

But more and more my mother came to believe that in order to thrive, we would have to leave the cocoon of Normal behind. So, with few resources and four children to care for, she decided to take a leap into the great unknown. I remember the day she announced that we were moving a thousand miles away to Fort Lauderdale. I was eleven and I listened doubtfully as she described how much we were going to love it there. We didn't know a single person in the area. But Mom had an infectious optimism and somehow she made our move feel like a grand adventure. Which, in the end, it turned out to be.

I had attended public school in Normal, but on the day we drove to the Pompano Beach middle school where I was to be registered, I couldn't help but gape at the plywood covering the windows, the graffiti spray-painted on the walls, and the police officers who patrolled the hallways. Florida's lack of a state income tax meant that schools were woefully underfunded. Mom and I walked only a few steps down the hall before I felt my arm being jerked. "Let's go," she said, pulling me back toward the entrance. "You deserve better than this."

After that, Mom was on a tear. We visited a local Catholic school but didn't feel so welcome, maybe because Mom was a divorced mother of four. After visits to other area private schools, we received news that, thanks to the great education I had received in Illinois, I was testing ahead of my grade level and had been offered a scholarship to a new school being started by the local Presbyterian church. Because it was a start-up, with no legacy to protect, it could take risks on a kid like me. I couldn't have imagined how that school would become the ticket to a great education that my mother never could have afforded, all thanks to the generosity of others.

At my new school, I was inspired and nurtured. I still remember my twenty-one-year-old sixth-grade teacher, Miss Neal, who made up excuses to run errands with me after class, which I later realized was her way of caring for a latchkey kid who was new to town. To this day she remains a very dear friend.

In the early years after we moved to the Fort Lauderdale area, I spent summers back in Illinois with my grandparents, growing closer to them with each passing year. When my grandmother died, I felt a huge loss, as did the rest of the family, but our spirits were lifted when my grandfather decided to buy a home and move just a few doors down from us. On my sixteenth birthday, I chose to move in with him on my own, and that experience led to a whole new education. Every day we had coffee together before school, and after school we'd talk about my day. Often we'd wander down the street to a canal where we'd go fishing together. I cherished my time with my grandfather, and he also instilled a self-discipline in me that I am grateful for to this day, including his habit of pounding on my bedroom door if I wasn't up by 7:00 a.m.—even on weekends or unscheduled summer days. With his deep voice and German accent, he'd loudly cry out through the door, "It's seven a.m.! Are you going to sleep all day?" I've often thought what he was really trying to convey was this: "It's a new day. There's much to be done. Don't waste it." And thanks to him, that is the spirit I've tried to carry through my life.

I had dreams of becoming a lawyer, and in high school I was lucky to land an internship with Judge E. Clay Shaw Jr., who would soon become mayor and then a member of Congress. Most of the work was administrative—filing, typing, and the like. But those afternoons in Judge Shaw's law office were my first exposure to a truly professional environment: people wore suits and spoke in a language and conducted themselves in a manner I'd not been previously exposed to. At the close of each week, Judge Shaw would call me into his office and sit me down on one of the two chairs flanking the fireplace (a rare sight in southern Florida) and query me: What was I working on? What had I learned that week? How were my grades? Was I staying on the straight and narrow? He was mentoring me, and each Friday, as I walked out of his office, I made a vow to never disappoint him.

During my college years, I volunteered on Shaw's campaign for Congress. After he was elected in 1980, I joined his team as a staff assistant while attending college classes at night. Thanks to this experience, I secured a job as a young political appointee in the Reagan administration when I moved to Washington. My oldest brother made the thousand-mile trip with me, lending me his Sears credit card once we'd arrived so I could splurge on an iron and ironing board. To this day, I speak to him nearly every morning. Mom didn't just raise a family; we were a tribe, always looking out for each other.

My career seemed to be on a positive trajectory, and it wasn't long before I found my way to the private sector. Those were the earliest days of the Internet, and the start-up that hired me was the nation's first pure play online service. I felt exhilarated working to democratize access to ideas, information, and communication— empowering people. When I was young, Mom had spent the better part of two years making monthly payments so I could have an encyclopedia set at home. Now all the knowledge contained in those vast volumes was accessible with the click of a button. It thrilled me to think that my role in the private sector could do more to benefit others than I might have achieved working in the public sector.

Before long I took a similar position at General Electric; and then, in my late twenties, I joined another young start-up that was to become America Online (AOL), where I'd spend nearly a decade as AOL helped usher in the Internet revolution. The name we chose for the service reflected our big idea: *getting America online*. At its peak, AOL carried 50 percent of the nation's Internet traffic. It was a richly rewarding experience. I felt incredibly lucky to be a part of one of the greatest periods of innovation the United States had seen.

It was during those AOL years that I added another significant and cherished role—I became a mom. My two daughters changed forever the way I see the world. Later, it was a blessing to expand to a blended family that added three more kids to the mix! I quickly realized that the role of working mom would require its own sense of fearlessness in the raising of children. What I couldn't have known then was just how much I would learn from them and what a source of inspiration they would be in my life.

As I had built my career and applied my skills to this point, it was always with a focus on empowering others. Yes, I had achieved more than I had hoped, but I was still restless, wanting to make an even bigger impact. So in 1997, I left AOL, and Steve and I cofounded the Case Foundation. I became the CEO. We made the commitment to give away the bulk of our wealth to benefit others, and for me it was an experience of coming full circle. As a former *beneficiary* of philanthropy, which had launched me into a world of opportunity, now I could help to lift others.

For me, the Case Foundation wasn't just about sharing the wealth. Family foundations are often the coda of a life successfully lived, a way to distribute money to worthy causes. But our vision for the Case Foundation was that it be a vibrant laboratory for change. It was the most ambitious quest of my life, and I could see how everything I'd done before helped to prepare me for the challenge.

I knew that becoming CEO of the Case Foundation was the first step of the most challenging endeavor of my life—one that required me to embrace a fearless mind-set, and that's what I've tried to do in the years since. More recently, after more than a decade of working on various boards at the National Geographic Society, I was privileged to be named the first female Chairman of the Board of Trustees. I have long loved this organization, which has been transforming people's lives for 130 years through the power of science, exploration, and storytelling. The fearless men and women of National Geographic have boldly gone to the front lines of the unknown, often at tremendous risk, and have shared their knowledge and experiences with the rest of us. And since adventures into the unknown require resources and a platform, the National Geographic Society makes that happen. Being a part of this remarkable organization, I felt my personal fearless quotient rising, and was happy to adopt Explorer-at-Large Jane Goodall's motto: "Every individual can make a difference every day." In fact, if you look closely at the National Geographic Society, you will see the five principles of Be Fearless at work every day across the organization and around the world.

Whether at the Case Foundation, at the National Geographic Society, or with any of the other initiatives and causes close to my heart, I am constantly reminded of my first and most enduring fearless role model. Mom passed away about a decade ago, but her generous nature and fierce determination continue to inspire me. She's the person who taught me to take risks, to see possibility, and to be good to others. She didn't use lofty words like "philanthropy," but she had an impact on everyone she touched. In this book, I talk about making a Big Bet. I realize that *I* was my mom's Big Bet; she devoted her life to helping me discover how to find purpose and success. From her, I learned that all of us can do great things, but sometimes it requires leaving the cocoon of Normal.

PART ONE

MAKE A BIG BET

Start right where you are

Be audacious

Burst through assumptions

Peek around corners

Now go, make your Big Bet

ONE

START RIGHT WHERE YOU ARE

On an afternoon in 2005, I sat in the waiting room of Dr. Barbara Van Dahlen's counseling office, fidgeting as the minutes ticked by. I had arrived early for my meeting with Barbara, a friend and family counselor with a kind heart and a reputation for excellence. My curiosity had been piqued when I'd seen her days earlier at an event and she'd asked if I might be willing to meet. "I have an idea," she'd said, "and I'd love to run it by you and see what you think." So there I sat, wondering what she might want to discuss.

Soon the door opened and Barbara warmly welcomed me into her office. "I have a problem," she started off. "And others in my profession are seeing the same thing." Week after week, she was getting calls for counseling services from men and women in the military and their families. With the war on terror raging in Afghanistan and Iraq, nearly 200,000 service personnel had been called to active duty, with many serving multiple tours. Barbara described to me the traumatic reality of life in such places. That trauma followed the soldiers home; there was a growing post-traumatic stress disorder (PTSD) crisis. And the stress of multiple tours of duty had taken a real toll on many military families. Unfortunately, she told me, the Department of Veterans Affairs was overwhelmed by the scope of the problem. It couldn't keep up with the demand for mental health services, leaving too many soldiers and their families without the resources they needed.

She told me that she'd personally taken on a few families pro bono and had convinced other colleagues to do the same. Giving just an hour a week of pro bono therapy wasn't too much of a hardship on any one doctor, and most of the doctors she'd talked to were happy to do their small part to help those on the front lines.

"So here's my idea," Barbara said. "I want to create a nationwide network of doctors and other caregivers who would agree to give an hour a week. If we can get enough of them to commit, we can help close the gap in mental health services for military families."

I sat absorbing what she was proposing before peppering her with questions about how she might go about setting up this national network, what kind of support she would need, and what kind of time frame was feasible. Finally, I asked the hardest question: Why did she, as a sole practitioner with no experience in organization building, think she could pull this off?

"Because the need is urgent, families are suffering, and I'm passionate about bringing a solution," she replied without hesitation.

Barbara's Big Bet was that she would be able to create a large enough network of doctors and caregivers—along with military, political, and private sector leaders—to be of assistance, and that her hook—"Give an Hour"—would appeal to people who wanted to make a difference but had limited time. I believed in Barbara's vision, and I left her office excited to be of help as she took the idea forward. It wasn't long before Give an Hour was born.

In the years since I sat in Barbara's office, thousands of providers across the country have answered her call. Nearly a quarter of a million hours have been donated by her network of licensed care providers, the equivalent of almost $25 million in counseling services—all free. In 2012, *Time* magazine named Barbara among the 100 Most Influential People in the World, and her organization has been given four stars, the highest ranking, by Charity Navigator, the nation's largest evaluator of charities, exceeding industry standards.

And Barbara hasn't stopped there. She has become a recognized leader in mental health, spearheading efforts to reduce the stigma and engaging high-profile entertainers to help carry her message and build an even broader movement. A documentary featuring her work aired on PBS in late 2017.

Barbara's story is a remarkable testament to what one individual can do to change the world. With no background in organization building, with no staff to support her, and without the funds and the network she knew she'd need, she made a Big Bet and took it one step at a time. In starting right where she was—one counselor giving an hour a week—she showed others that they could do the same. She asked only for the smallest commitment, and the enthusiastic response was a tribute to the soundness of her plan.

The challenge to start right where you are is the great equalizer. For the most part, the public doesn't hear about Big Bets until their results are out in the world, proven and successful. But if we could peek back to the beginning, we'd often find ourselves amazed by the simplicity of their origins. This should be inspiring for those of us who want to make a difference but feel thwarted by a lack of experience or resources.

This applies to innovation and invention as well. In America, we think of an innovator as that lone guy tinkering in a garage who has an "aha!" moment. And while that might make for good storytelling, the truth is that it's very seldom how breakthroughs come to be. Time and time again, they come from people living with real frustrations, who get to a point where they realize, "There has to be a better way." So they set out to create one. Take, for instance, "newfangled" ideas like dishwashers, home security devices, and windshield wipers—none invented by lone guys in garages. In fact, all were invented by women.

A striking example of this dynamic came more than one hundred years ago when an extraordinarily successful female entrepreneur built an enterprise, also based on a problem that needed solving. That woman was Madam C.J. Walker, the daughter of slaves, who had the courage and initiative to launch her entrepreneurial dream and make a difference in spite of the extreme hardship of her life. The story of her Big Bet is so compelling that in 2018 LeBron James's production company announced plans to create a limited series about her, starring Oscar winner Octavia Spencer.

We can only imagine the level of challenge Walker experienced in her early years. She was born Sarah Breedlove in 1867, just after the Civil War, on a plantation in Louisiana, where her parents and all of her siblings had been slaves. Although she was free, her early life was marked by tragedy and struggle. She lost both parents by the age of seven and was sent to live with her sister and her husband in Mississippi, who hired her out as domestic help when she was only ten. At fourteen she married in order to flee their abusive home. By age seventeen she was a mother, and she was widowed at twenty. She worked as a washerwoman for $1.50 a week, and there was little indication that her life would take such a dramatic turn. She did not live in a climate like today's where entrepreneurial dreams can often come true. Opportunity seemed out of reach for a poor woman with no resources. But as she would later say, "I got my start by giving myself a start."

Like many Big Bets, Breedlove's originated in an effort to solve a personal problem—her hair was falling out, and she could find no products on the market to address her condition. At the time, scalp disease and subsequent baldness were common for black women, largely due to harsh chemicals used for washing. Rather than accept her plight, she set out to experiment with her own homemade concoctions, aided by advice from her barber brothers. She adopted a regimen of daily scalp washing with a hair solution she had created. With her daily use of her new formula, her hair grew back, and she began to look at ways her unique formula could help other women.

When Breedlove married journalist Charles Joseph Walker, becoming known as Madam C.J. Walker, she took her "Madam Walker's Wonderful Hair Grower" product and "Walker System" and began going door to door, teaching women about hair treatment and the use of her product. Along with her husband, she set out across the country to build new markets for her growing hair-care business. In the process, her effort became so much more than selling a product. By training and recruiting large numbers of young black women across the country as a sales force—a remarkable feat early in the twentieth century—she empowered and generated income for women who themselves had few opportunities. She created the Madam C.J. Walker Hair Culturists Union, with dues of twenty-five cents per month, to provide business and educational opportunities, as well as life insurance and other benefits. She encouraged this network of young entrepreneurs to practice philanthropy in their communities, and at her annual convention that brought them together, she provided special recognition for those who'd been most generous in their communities back home. "I am not satisfied in making money for myself," she said. "I endeavor to provide employment to hundreds of women of my race."

Madam Walker only lived to the age of fifty-one, and in the final decade of her life she became a popular motivational speaker, millionaire, and philanthropist. "I had to make my own living and my own opportunity," she told her audiences. "But I made it! Don't sit down and wait for the opportunities to come. Get up and make them." Madam Walker did more than create a product. She would say that her Big Bet was the opportunity she created for others.

> *"I got my start by giving myself a start."*
> —MADAM C.J. WALKER

Sometimes starting where you are means already having a core of knowledge and experience, as Barbara Van Dahlen did. But sometimes, in this era of disruption, Big Bets can come from people who arrived at their inventions without preconceived notions or any experience at all.

In the late 1990s, Brian Chesky and Joe Gebbia, recent graduates of the Rhode Island School of Design, struck out for San Francisco, where so many young professionals were flocking to at the time. But soon enough, the high cost of living had them struggling to pay the rent. They knew they needed to find a way to get some extra income—and fast. At about the same time, they heard grumblings that a big design conference coming to the city had bought out nearly all the nearby hotel rooms, leaving many attendees without a place to stay. What if, they asked themselves, we rent out some space in our apartment? They created a simple website with pictures of their loft and the three air mattresses they had purchased to "rent out." Renters were promised a home-cooked breakfast as part of the deal. It didn't take long to get the first booking—a recent graduate from Arizona State University desperate for an affordable place to stay. (Brian and Joe charged eighty dollars per mattress.) Soon two other conference attendees confirmed their reservations. Airbnb was born.

The small success of their venture motivated Brian and Joe to turn the idea into something more permanent. They boldly began to solicit investors, most of whom thought the idea of staying in the home of a stranger was crazy. Their timing wasn't so great either. The looming financial crisis was dampening investors' appetite for backing untested ideas.

To keep their endeavor afloat, Brian and Joe devised a clever twist on the breakfast part of the plan. Trying to get a foothold in Denver, which was hosting the 2008 Democratic National Convention, they had the idea to market signature cereal boxes as a way to create buzz and extra revenue around the convention, which they later duplicated at the Republican Convention in Saint Paul, Minnesota. Obama O's and Cap'n McCain cereals became a hit, providing $30,000 of much-needed income.

In January 2009, Airbnb was accepted into the competitive Y Combinator accelerator program for start-ups, which came with a $20,000 investment from Y Combinator's cofounder Paul Graham. Graham hadn't been too impressed with the idea of someone paying to sleep on an air mattress on a stranger's floor. But as the two young entrepreneurs prepared to leave their first interview with him, Joe gave Graham a box of Obama O's. "Wow," said Graham. "You guys are like cockroaches. You just won't die. If you can convince people to pay forty dollars for a box of cereal, you can probably convince them to pay to sleep on each other's air mattresses." The cereal sealed the deal.

Airbnb didn't hire a big team, or spend big money on marketing and advertising. In effect, Brian and Joe asked: *What is the least amount of time or effort we can spend on an experiment to determine if this idea will fly?* They learned to stay nimble and to identify opportunities to keep afloat until they were established.

> *"One of my biggest strengths was precisely how little I knew."*
> —BRIAN CHESKY

The growth process wasn't without problems. When you introduce a new concept, some people are bound to resist. There was intense lobbying from the hotel industry. Some communities and apartment buildings blocked owners from renting their spaces with Airbnb, and people worried about strangers trashing their homes. But the idea caught on because it touched on something travelers were looking for. It wasn't just a matter of price. It was the sense of belonging somewhere, of staying in a place that felt more welcoming than a sterile hotel room. It also provided homeowners grappling with high property taxes and empty nests an easy way of earning income. Today the company operates in more than 80,000 cities and 191 countries. Over half a million people stay in one of Airbnb's more than 3 million listings every day.

• • •

So, you see, anyone can make a Big Bet, and getting started often begins with a simple question: "Why not me?" Imagine being a college student. (Maybe you *are* one and don't have to imagine.) Your daily life is filled with classes and activities, family and friends. What would compel you to also take on a project such as ending hunger on college campuses? That's what UCLA students Rachel Sumekh and Bryan Pezeshki did. Their national nonprofit organization, Swipe Out Hunger, began in 2010 as a grassroots initiative after Bryan noticed a call for food donations and asked some friends, "Who wants to help?" When Rachel responded, she was disturbed to find that she was the only one. The following Saturday, she and Bryan spent five hours moving donated food across the campus for distribution to students who couldn't afford to eat.

The problem they set out to tackle wasn't a new one, but it certainly went unacknowledged for years. While we don't think of students on college campuses going hungry, my own experience is a personal testament to this. Although I was a recipient of financial aid during my college years, the aid did not cover a meal plan. With the meager amount of money I had earned mostly going to books and other extra costs not covered by financial aid, I often had to skip meals because I simply didn't have the funds. I was fortunate because close family friends who lived nearby invited me to dinner routinely and often sent me back to my dorm with leftovers for lunch the next day. (I grow a bit teary as I reflect on this—how lucky I was to have so many in my life whose generosity and loving care were transformative in big ways and small.)

Today an estimated one in seven college students nationwide is considered so "food insecure" they've visited a food bank; in some states, that number rises to one in four. Which is where Swipe Out Hunger comes in. Rachel and Bryan's effort started with a sign, to-go boxes, and some encouragement to fellow students to collect extra food. But it wasn't long before they came up against dining hall management, which felt threatened by what they considered competition. One dining manager even smashed Rachel's boxes and shouted, "Get this program the hell off my campus."

It was clear that Swipe Out Hunger needed another way forward, which was when Rachel and Bryan set their sights on the college meal plan. At many schools, it's easy enough for those parents who can afford it to load money onto what's a bit like an ATM card for food each September, which students can swipe each time they enjoy an on-campus meal. It's not uncommon to end up with money left on the card at the end of the year, and most schools don't allow that balance to roll over to the following year.

Unused meal plan credits can reach hundreds of thousands of dollars at bigger universities. What if, Rachel wondered, students could "swipe" to donate unused meal credits to students in need? It was a brilliant idea—and so simple—and should have been widely embraced. But faced with the loss of so much revenue, UCLA didn't make it easy. As Rachel later said: "We felt like kids breaking the rules." The founders persisted, however, and by 2012 Swipe Out Hunger had achieved such acclaim that their efforts were recognized by the White House, who named the student leaders Champions for Change. President Barack Obama himself congratulated the fifteen students who came from California to receive the honor.

After graduation, the students went their separate ways, Rachel into social work. But before long, the Swipe Out Hunger team, which had always been staffed by volunteers, decided it needed a full-time head to run the growing nonprofit. Rachel suggested it should be her. "You're too nice to be a leader," a male acquaintance told her. But Rachel didn't take the comment to heart. Today, under Rachel's lead, the program has expanded to thirty campuses across the country, built along a franchise model that enables student leaders to feel a strong sense of ownership. The program has delivered more than 1.3 million meals to students in need, and now includes food pantries, including one at UCLA, where a student can walk in and grab what is needed, with no stigma attached. In June 2017, the governor of California signed into law legislation to incentivize universities across the state to adopt the program, approving a $7.5 million budget to move toward "hunger-free campuses."

Students often send Rachel notes expressing gratitude. One young woman said she wouldn't have enrolled in college had the program not been available, since like so many students, she received financial aid but did not have a way to pay for food. Rachel likes to say that the cost of a meal is small, but the cost to society of someone dropping out of school or not enrolling is enormous. "College students have a lot of insecurities," she reminds people. "Food shouldn't be one of them."

Much like Rachel Sumekh, Shazi Visram, the daughter of Pakistani and Tanzanian immigrants, got her idea for a healthy baby food brand when she was an MBA student at Columbia University. She wasn't a mother then, but she was moved by the story of a classmate, a working mother of two, who complained about her lack of baby food options; she didn't have time for homemade baby

food, but wished she could find something with healthy ingredients. Shazi, who admits to having boundless confidence, instilled
by her parents, decided to tackle the problem. She studied the market and polled her friends who were parents, and was amazed to
find that the baby food market had remained stalled for decades,
even as the population was growing increasingly interested in organic foods with healthful ingredients. She decided that was going
to be her Big Bet.

Finding investors was the hardest part—she was still in school.
But with an initial investment from her mother of $20,000, she
went on to raise half a million dollars, enough to launch her food
company, Happy Family, in 2006. There were some starts and stops
along the way. Initially, her product was frozen, but she found that
people didn't shop for baby food in the frozen food section of the
supermarket. So she changed course in 2009, with pouches that
could be stored on shelves in the baby food sections. The product
rapidly took off from there.

This is, of course, the short version of Shazi's story. Behind
the scenes, there were years of research, testing, and searching for
investors. She didn't have deep pockets or family connections, so
seeking investors was a big part of her job in the early years. In the
beginning, she had to sell the idea to mostly male investors—not
exactly the prime audience for a mom-friendly product. Eventually,
though, she found response from a new class of impact investors—
a phenomenon we'll discuss later in this book. These investors were
not only attracted to the clear success of Shazi's company, but to
the opportunity to do something good for the health of children.
In 2013, Shazi sold her company to Danone, a Paris-based mul-
tinational company committed to products that promote health.

Her early investors realized a 30x return. She remains CEO, but has also become an investor in other companies looking to do good. Her broader mission is to do everything she can to promote the health and well-being of babies and young children. The urgency increased after she became a mother. When Shazi's son was diagnosed with autism, her life's work and personal life converged. Today her mission is expanding to the health of the whole family, with products for older children and pregnant women. Her perspective is simple: she is only interested in projects that will help change the world for the better. And although Happy Family is very profitable, she would also say, "Babies before profits."

• • •

Starting right where you are can be the mantra for every visionary. And it always reminds me of a lesson I took away from Jen, an athletic trainer I worked with one summer to push my physical boundaries. Jen is young and remarkably fit. She's won many triathlons and she inspired me (and perhaps intimidated me too) the summer we trained together. I'd boxed and trained for my black belt in Tae Kwon Do, but I had never run a race or run distances in a mountain setting. But that summer I was staying at a farm in the mountains of Virginia surrounded by very hilly, winding country roads. By the end of the summer, I wanted to be able to run the three miles of roads—hills and all. For most runners, three miles is no big deal, but I had never run a race or even up and down hills.

Jen's first piece of advice was: "Break it down into chunks." She told me, "Only look at the next three feet in front of you, because if you look a mile down the road, you'll say, 'I'm never going to make it.' But you can always make it three more feet." And she was right. Eventually three more feet extended to the next mailbox, and then to the bend in the road—each distance just a little farther than before. By the end of the summer, I had gone from running in spurts of just a few minutes to running the full three miles of hills.

There's wisdom in the "chunk it" approach for Big Bets too. Like everything else in life, big achievements often start with small steps; take enough small steps, and you can do powerful things. So I invite you to think about how to break "impossible" things into chunks.

And there is another lesson Jen taught me that applies to any Be Fearless effort: One day, well into the training, I was really having a hard time. I'd noticed that some days I felt like I could fly, and other days every step was a struggle. "That's how it is for me even after my triathlon wins," Jen said. "Some days are hard, some days are easy. But you just keep going." I took that as a challenge for life more broadly: some days are just harder than others to stay on task, to dig deep to find inner reserves, and to keep moving toward your goal. The key is to remind yourself that tomorrow will likely be easier.

I've often thought about how Big Bets that change the world can start as Big Bets in one's personal life. Watching my mother struggle to provide for our family, I understood at a young age how challenging that could be. Some days I would only see my mom for the hour between when I came home from school and when she left for the night shift. So I made a Big Bet early in life to create enough financial security for myself that I could have some flexibility in my career once I started a family. With all decisions guided by this central idea, it wasn't so hard to ask for a raise, because I was on a mission.

I also committed at an early age to using my time and talents to empower others, as being a kid on full scholarship at a private school opened my eyes to the differences in opportunities life can present. I originally imagined working as a lawyer in the public sector. But, interestingly, the winding road of life led me instead to a private sector career in technology, where I had the privilege of helping to empower millions of people through the digital revolution and the Internet. This, in turn, gave me the resources to build a foundation that today invests in people and ideas that can change the world. I'm not sure I would have risked leaving the public sector for the private if I hadn't had the inner conviction that I would stay focused on my big goal of helping others, no matter what.

Do you have a Big Bet or a big idea that's been burning inside you? What would it look like for you to start right where you are and take your own Big Bet forward? Each of the stories in this chapter demonstrates that launching a Big Bet doesn't require a large budget, proven expertise, or the underpinning of a large company or organization. What it does require is the ability to assess what you have *now* that you can leverage in your current situation to advance your idea. Start there.

TWO

BE AUDACIOUS

I was too young to remember the day President John F. Kennedy announced that America was going to the moon, but I do recall growing up in a world where the idea of a moonshot existed— as well as Kennedy's memorable words that we were doing these things "not because they are easy, but because they are hard." While the term "moonshot" is now used to describe any big, bold effort, I wonder if we grasp just how bold President Kennedy's Big Bet was in 1961.

Landing on the moon was a huge long shot. Americans were ill-equipped to even imagine such a feat. At the time the president declared his commitment, we didn't have the materials needed to build the rockets, let alone the technology and lightweight components for a spaceship that could make it to the moon. We didn't have the capability to reduce the size of the systems required to fit in such a cramped space, nor the advanced communications to keep track of the capsule in space. We didn't even have the math or the physics know-how to tell us how to shoot a spaceship up there and get it back. But, as President Kennedy said, "We choose to go to the moon in this decade." *We choose*. And we did.

We don't always appreciate how many of the things we enjoy in our lives today are a direct result of the original moonshot challenge. This includes satellite communications, global weather systems, plastics that can endure harsh environments, the miniaturization of technology (1960s computers were too large to fit on a spacecraft), and even the math formulas required for proper rocket trajectories out of and back into the atmosphere. President Kennedy doesn't get much credit today when we pick up our iPhones and use GPS or check the weather or send an email, but these innovations owe much to his Big Bet.

What I keep coming back to about President Kennedy's moonshot is how audacious it was. Big Bets are the engine for countless other innovations. They can change a culture, a geography, a mindset, and a political system. The evidence is clear: to make a better world, we have to take bigger risks and make bigger bets.

Like most people who were alive to witness the actual moonshot, the event on July 20, 1969, has special resonance for me. It remains one of my most cherished memories. I was a little kid, and when my mom woke me from sleep to tell me the moment had arrived, I sprang out of bed and rushed to join the rest of the family in front of the glowing television set in our living room. The image on the screen was that of famed news anchor Walter Cronkite. Then it happened—a somewhat blurry black-and-white image of astronaut Neil Armstrong descending down the ladder of the lunar landing craft to place the first human foot on the moon. It felt as though our nation, and the people of the whole world, gave a collective gasp. When the American flag was planted on the surface of the moon, our family erupted in a cheer. This truly was history in the making. Even at that young age, I felt the fearlessness of the expedition.

In the days that followed, I got an astronaut lunchbox and thermos, which I proudly displayed in the lunchroom. I wanted to be just like those brave men who had boldly gone where no one had before. The influence on pop culture and consumer products—and the inspiration they represented—was everywhere. My own lunchbox was packed with new "space food" such as Space Food Sticks and Tang—the same powdered orange juice the astronauts drank in space!

Countless youth like myself were motivated by the realization of JFK's bold dream. Recognizing that audacity, we saw that we could be audacious too. Imagine doing something that could so inspire young people today.

> *"Remember to look up at the stars and not down at your feet."*
> —STEPHEN HAWKING

Few modern organizations embody this idea as well as Google X (now called simply X), the self-designated "moonshot factory" opened in 2010. It's a place of almost unlimited inventiveness, described by Derek Thompson in the *Atlantic* as "a think-tank panel with the instincts of an improv troupe." But it's much more than that.

Leading this venture is Astro Teller, whose first name would seem to have fated his life to have something special in store. (In fact, his given name was Eric.) Add to his name a remarkable lineage—his two grandfathers were Gérard Debreu, a Nobel Prize–winning economist, and Edward Teller, known as the "father of the hydrogen bomb" for his extraordinary contributions in nuclear and molecular physics—and elite academic credentials, and you might find yourself somewhat in awe to be seated next to him at dinner, as I was at a conference when we first met. But the engaging, bearded innovator who leads X surprised me with his openness. He encourages "low deference to authority," he told me, and while his goals may be stratospheric, his style is approachable and exuberant.

X works by tackling projects with a simple three-point blueprint: (1) find a mammoth problem that affects millions or even billions of people; (2) propose a radical solution; (3) have a reason to believe that the technology necessary for this radical solution is possible.

X strives to mix things up. "You'll find an aerospace engineer working alongside a fashion designer and former military ops commanders brainstorming with laser experts," Astro once told a TED audience. "These inventors, engineers, and makers are dreaming up technologies that we hope can make the world a wonderful place." One of Astro's basic principles is to create an environment of discovery that starts from people's passions "instead of putting people in a place that already exists and making sure they don't color outside the lines."

A lot of X's business happens in secret, but among its better-known efforts is Project Loon, which works to create balloon-powered Internet for everyone. Astro calls it X's "craziest" project, yet it was successfully deployed in Puerto Rico in 2017 after Hurricane Maria. The X method is to work on a project until it either fails or "graduates" to become an independent Google business. One of X's graduate businesses is Waymo, which grew from Google's self-driving car project. We'll return to X later to explore its remarkable model of achieving greatness from failure. But suffice it to say that as Big Bets go, X is breaking the mold every day.

• • •

It could be said that the very founding of America was a Big Bet: the fearless idea that control could be wrested from what was then the most powerful nation in the world by a motley citizens' army, and that this people's rebellion could form a new nation based on principles of freedom, equality, peace, and prosperity. It would have been so easy for our founders to have continued negotiating their individual grievances with the British as just another colony looking for incremental concessions. Instead, they chose to start a revolution that would honor their convictions and invent a new form of government.

This is the Big Bet way of thinking: it's not just about developing a product but about opening up whole new territories for exploration. That's why when an innovator like Elon Musk talks about SpaceX, he'll acknowledge the company's many incremental efforts, but he never fails to remind the world that he is on a mission to send humans to Mars—and to do so by 2030. His goal with SpaceX and Tesla is "redefining how we travel on earth and in space." This is the essence of a Big Bet: an audacious, unifying goal by which anyone can be inspired and around which people can coalesce. And when SpaceX launched its rocket in January 2018, the first big test of Elon's "crazy" dream was proven out. There are plenty who predict that Elon will stumble, run out of cash, or fall short of his vision, and there are many questions and understandable criticisms about his methods, his brashness, and the way he engages detractors. But, despite those valid concerns, there are lessons to be learned from the way Elon is able to fully identify and apply the lessons of failure in pursuing his vision.

We live in a time of incredible audacity. And it's exciting to see how much of this is coming from young people. To be sure, young people know how to be loud; they know how to be disruptive. But it's impressive to see that they also know how to organize and promote their causes. Think of the Parkland #NeverAgain movement, which has broken through the typical trajectory that follows a gun violence tragedy—brief national outrage and then, within weeks, back to business as usual. Taking on the NRA in social media and a massive March on Washington, the student leaders who emerged after the February 14, 2018, shooting at Marjory Stoneman Douglas High School in Parkland, Florida, have demanded universal background checks, raising the minimum age for gun purchases to twenty-one, and a ban on assault weapons. They've also vowed to oppose elected officials who receive large donations from the NRA. Their efforts could be seen when conservative Florida Governor Rick Scott signed into law a ban on automatic weapons—a historic change that could only have been achieved by people with a Big Bet in mind.

> *"I am not afraid. . . . I was born to do this."*
> —JOAN OF ARC

Parkland isn't the first time we've seen students enter the fray. Indeed, we continue to be inspired by the next generation of emerging leaders. After hosting a national competition, the Case Foundation received an entry from a young woman named Jordyn Schara, who wrote: "I am Fearless because at 14, when our government refused to take action, I created my own 501(c)(3) nonprofit to start a community service project that sets up 24/7 drug collection programs." Jordyn's idea came after she discovered that more than 2.1 million youth ages twelve to seventeen abuse prescription drugs. She wanted to provide a way for these drugs to be taken off the streets and disposed of in a safe, environmentally friendly way. So she set up drug collection containers at local Wisconsin police stations, distributed flyers, and gave talks to spread awareness.

It wasn't easy for a young girl to get the attention of the people who could help her realize her vision. When she learned that a state grant was available to help communities start drug collection programs, she asked her town's grant writer if he would apply. He turned her down. Undeterred, she took her request to a nearby community, and although they agreed to apply for the grant, they told her they wouldn't share the money. So fourteen-year-old Jordyn decided to apply on her own. She was stunned when she won the grant, but then she did something even more remarkable. She told the two towns that had rejected her that she was splitting the grant money with them.

In its first four years, Jordyn's Wisconsin Prescription Pill and Drug Disposal (WIP2D2) program collected more than 600,000 pounds of prescription drugs. Since its founding in 2008, the program has started eleven drug collection programs and helped keep more than 1.5 million pounds of drugs away from young children and teens. Jordyn was a winner of the Case Foundation's 2012 Finding Fearless challenge and has since graduated from the University of Wisconsin–Madison, where she majored in broadcast journalism and gender and women's studies.

• • •

If I told you that someone could change the world with a brownie-baking company, you might have your doubts. But then, you haven't met the changemaker who started Greyston Bakery. Bernie Glassman was a well-known American Buddhist and social activist seeking ways to stop the cycle of poverty in his community when he opened Greyston Bakery in Yonkers, New York, in 1982 to create jobs without regard to education, prior employment, or deal breakers such as a history of incarceration, homelessness, or drug use. In thirty-six years, what started as a modest enterprise has grown into a world-class manufacturer, producing tons (literally!) of brownies and cookies annually for companies such as Ben & Jerry's, Whole Foods, and Delta Airlines.

To this day, Greyston uses open hiring: anyone from anywhere can walk in and put their name down on a list, and when a new position opens up, replacements are chosen according to who signed up first. As Greyston CEO and president Mike Brady says, "We don't hire people to bake brownies, we bake brownies to hire people." Greyston has also expanded operations to become a community leader, with major outreach programs including a workforce development program, the Greyston Community Gardens, and launched an effort to teach other companies how to incorporate open hiring into their practices. The story of Greyston Bakery reminds us that Big Bets can start in the sweetest and most unexpected ways.

This kind of thinking is how change can happen in the United States and worldwide.

• • •

"If Chile can do it, you can do it!" Those were the words of Michelle Bachelet, the former president of Chile, upon receiving the

National Geographic Planetary Leadership Award in Washington, DC, in June 2018. It was only the night before that, as Chairman of the National Geographic Society, I had hosted President Bachelet for dinner. Bachelet served as president of Chile from 2006 to 2010 and 2014 to 2018. Due to term limits in Chile, the terms were not consecutive. When she was elected for her second term, she won an impressive 62 percent of the vote. But it wasn't always obvious that her life would lead her to such influence and achievement. Growing up, Bachelet was the daughter of a respected military officer in Chile. Following a coup d'état by General Augusto Pinochet in 1973, Bachelet's father was imprisoned and tortured for working for President Salvador Allende; he died in prison after a year. Bachelet and her mother were detained, threatened, and eventually exiled. Years later, when she was finally given permission to return to her homeland, Bachelet served as a tireless activist for the return of democracy to Chile, all the while completing her studies, and eventually becoming a surgeon. This led to her role as minister of health, and later as minister of national defense, before she was elected to Chile's highest office.

Bachelet has compiled an impressive biography of contributions to her nation, often against great odds. But the one for which she was being feted by the National Geographic Society was also a gift to the planet. Under her presidential leadership, five new national parks were created, expanding Chile's network of parks to cover more than 10 million acres—including a truly extraordinary effort led by Kristine Tompkins, who along with her late husband, Doug Tompkins, preserved and then handed over slightly more than a million acres of land to Chile. In March 2018, inspired by the work of National Geographic's Pristine Seas initiative, Bachelet created nine marine reserves to protect biodiversity, increasing marine protected areas from 4.2 percent of Chile's sea surface when she took office to 42.4 percent when she left, representing more than 540,000 square miles of protected marine life.

When asked about her leadership, which serves as a true model for conservation, President Bachelet said, "We demonstrate that it is not necessary to be a rich country to promote an environmental agenda that makes a difference."

The nature of Big Bets is that they are audacious at their initiation. If you've ever had a bright idea you wanted to take forward but some voice inside you said, "I could never do *that*," check yourself. Big, audacious ideas become a reality by taking a thousand small steps. What often seems impossible at the start becomes more plausible with each new action taken toward the goal.

THREE

BURST THROUGH ASSUMPTIONS

There is a special photo on the wall at the entrance to my office that hangs there for all to see. It's a photo of an eighty-plus-year-old Eunice Kennedy Shriver, the founder of the Special Olympics, in a pool with some of the athletes. She looks joyful. At the bottom of the photo, she inscribed these words: "Jean, I want you in the pool with me next summer!" Sadly, before the next summer came along, Eunice died.

I never did have the chance to literally get in the pool with Eunice, but I was lucky enough to know, and build great affection for, this remarkable leader in her later years, and the Case Foundation partnered with the Special Olympics to help them expand their international presence. Eunice's work has inspired me to reach further, to aim higher, to take risks, and to never forget about those who are most vulnerable—to see the promise and the possibilities in everyone. "Get in the pool with me" is an invitation that constantly reminds me to jump in the pool of life and make a difference.

To understand Eunice, you need to know her story. It was a hot, humid summer day in Chicago in 1968 when Eunice convened the first Special Olympics Games. Just seven weeks earlier, her younger brother Senator Robert Kennedy had been assassinated, his loss fol-

lowing the tragic early deaths of three other of Eunice's siblings, including President John Kennedy. Her mission in Chicago that day
was inspired by her sister Rosemary, who had been born with an intellectual disability. As children, Eunice and Rosemary played sports
together and formed a close bond. Eunice made it her mission to empower people with disabilities through sports. Beginning as a summer program called Camp Shriver in her backyard, by 1968 Eunice's
movement had expanded across the United States and into Canada.

Eunice was passionately focused on a Big Bet: change the world
through sports—which was what brought her to Chicago that summer. There, as the sun beat down on the thousand athletes assembled
at Soldier Field, Eunice recited the Special Olympics athlete's oath:

> *Let me win, but if I cannot win*
> *let me be brave in the attempt.*

On the field that day, Eunice boldly announced her belief that
someday 1 million individuals with intellectual disabilities would
compete in these games, which seemed like an audacious goal in
1968. Who could have predicted that decades later, that number
would grow to more than 5 million athletes once incorrectly labeled as incapable of thriving, who would participate in annual
competitions in 170 countries around the globe?

Eunice's dream was to promote dignity for all, and over the
years the Special Olympics mission has expanded to include a robust set of activities to change attitudes and bring resources, such
as schooling, medical care, and job prospects, to the intellectually
challenged across the world. It is widely recognized that opportunity and basic human rights have been transformed because of the

movement started in Eunice's backyard. What began as an effort to reach out to a few children in need forever transformed the way societies regarded those with disabilities.

One such athlete was Loretta Claiborne, one of seven children born to a mother who was on welfare. Doctors told her mother Loretta wouldn't live long, and recommended that she be institutionalized because of her severe intellectual disabilities. But her mother would have none of it. She took her daughter home and tirelessly advocated for her, always on the lookout for opportunities. One of them, the Special Olympics, changed Loretta's life—and, by extension, the lives of countless others.

Today Loretta is recognized as a world-class runner and gifted motivational speaker who happens to have an intellectual disability. She has completed twenty-six marathons (her best time is 3:03), has a fourth-degree black belt in karate, is fluent in five languages (including American Sign Language), is the recipient of two honorary doctorate degrees, was the subject of a Walt Disney movie titled *The Loretta Claiborne Story*, has appeared twice on *Oprah*, and has spoken in front of presidents and Congress on numerous occasions. "I figured if my story could change a person's mind about another person, or especially a child's mind about another child, then it was the right thing to do," Loretta says.

Loretta is perfectly comfortable speaking to presidents and before Congress. Once, at a White House event in the East Room that was full of dignitaries, she spoke before I did. Her speech was so powerful that I was a bit dismayed at having to follow her. She is unique in her ability to inspire.

Thanks to their own fearlessness, and allies like Eunice Shriver, Loretta and other athletes have been able to burst through the assumptions that leave too many people with disabilities on the sidelines. But every Special Olympics athlete who has achieved physical excellence first had to reject the doubts that had been planted in his or her own mind. Making a Big Bet can sometimes start by changing the way people—and oftentimes you yourself—think about the potential for one person to make a difference.

> *"The most effective way to do it is to do it."*
> —AMELIA EARHART

As for Eunice, if you visit Washington, DC, and find yourself walking near the White House, don't be surprised if you see a large medallion on the sidewalk in recognition of her extraordinary life and contributions. The Points of Light Monument walkway is known as the "Extra Mile" in Washington, honoring actions and commitments to service that have transformed our nation and the world. The Case Foundation considered it an honor to sponsor this tribute to Eunice, a true model of the Be Fearless spirit and actions.

• • •

Whenever I am in or near an ocean, my mind turns to a hero of the ocean, my friend and National Geographic Explorer-in-Residence Enric Sala. I still remember the first time I heard him speak. I sat transfixed as I listened to a young Enric, with his ponytail, Spanish accent, and passionate voice, describing his commitment to helping protect and save some of the last pristine marine ecosystems in the world. His Big Bet: work with governments to establish twenty marine protected areas (MPAs) by 2020, including some of the most wild and remote pristine areas of our seas.

Enric's inspiration for his Big Bet derived from his previous role as a professor at Scripps Institution of Oceanography in La Jolla, California. Having published numerous papers highlighting the fragile state of marine ecosystems, Enric says, he realized he was "writing the obituary of the ocean." Oceans make up more than 70 percent of the earth's surface, and Enric knew that restoring and protecting key portions of the ocean would not only help save the natural habitats and species, but that the oceans play a vital role in providing over 50 percent of the oxygen we breathe and absorbing over one-third of the carbon pollution in the air. As marine experts often say, "The ocean is the lungs of our planet."

So he decided to act. Knowing that the work of establishing new MPAs would require collaboration with governments around the world, he joined National Geographic and outlined his plan. Then, one by one, he burst through assumptions and beliefs that getting governments to cooperate would just be too hard. He likes to say, "First I help them fall in love with the ocean, then I talk to them about what it takes to protect these amazing places."

To date, more than eighteen sites have been established as new MPAs, constituting more than 5 million square kilometers of our oceans. Enric has brought a highly collaborative approach to his efforts, engaging a diverse set of stakeholders and organizations. With the last MPAs within sight, Enric is close to seeing his Big Bet become a reality—and with it a renewed consciousness that our oceans matter and are worthy of protection.

I saw Enric's strategy play out firsthand when I joined him for an expedition to a pristine area known as the Gardens of the Queens, located off the coast of Cuba. For five days we went diving three times a day. The joint team of Cubans and Americans conducted fish counts as part of the dives and evaluated the health of the reefs. Although I had fallen in love with the ocean at a tender age, the passion that stirred within me while diving in this pristine site moved me to the point of tears behind my diving mask. It was as though I were witnessing the ocean from a time gone by, before human activity degraded the health of reefs. I am five foot five and at one point I had a goliath grouper swim by me that far exceeded my height. Large predators, including sharks, were abundant in these waters—many more than I had ever seen in one place. In that trip I witnessed firsthand Enric's ability to move people to do all they can to protect these precious places on our planet.

• • •

Many big ideas begin with an understanding of what doesn't work, and new breakthroughs often benefit from what's been tried before— good news for all of us who think, "I'm not creative enough." Sara Blakely was getting ready for a party and wanted the shaping effect of pantyhose beneath her pants but without the feet because she was wearing sandals. She took a pair of scissors and cut off the feet, and that was the inspiration for Spanx. With no experience in fashion design or manufacturing—she sold fax machines for a living—Sara set out in her free time to learn everything she could, even travel- ing to visit manufacturing plants. One day early on, speaking to a doubtful buyer at Neiman Marcus, she took the (female) buyer into the bathroom to demonstrate her product. Neiman Marcus became her first client, Oprah Winfrey announced Spanx as one of her "favorite things," and Sara was off. Today the company Sara started with a $5,000 investment generates sales in the hundreds of millions annually, and she has become a leading philanthropist for female entrepreneurs. "Don't be intimidated by what you don't know," Sara advises. "That can be your greatest strength and ensure that you do things differently from everyone else."

Sara is an example of the rigorous entrepreneurial spirit we see everywhere. In our work with changemakers across the nation, we at the Case Foundation have come to appreciate that there are many arenas left for disruption—many status quos ready to be shaken up. I recall sitting across from two young entrepreneurs at the annual SXSW conference in Austin several years back. It was a beautiful, sunny afternoon, but we were spending our day in a hotel meeting space, with what felt like a revolving door of entrepreneurs coming through. But David Gilboa and Neil Blumenthal really stood out. They had an idea for shaking up a well-established business sector: eyeglasses.

David and Neil were MBA students at the Wharton School when the cash-strapped David lost his eyeglasses and had to pay $700 for replacements. That got them thinking: Could there be a better way? Neil had previously worked for a nonprofit, Vision-Spring, that trained poor women in the developing world to start businesses offering eye exams and selling glasses that were affordable to people making less than four dollars a day. He had helped expand the nonprofit's presence to ten countries, supporting thousands of female entrepreneurs and boosting the organization's staff from two to thirty. At the time, it hadn't occurred to Neil that an idea birthed in the nonprofit sector could be transferred to the private sector. But later at Wharton, as he and David considered entering the eyeglass business, after being shocked by the high cost of replacing David's glasses, they decided they were out to build more than a company—they were on a social mission as well.

They asked a simple question: Why had no one ever sold eye-glasses online? Well, because some believed it was *impossible*. For one thing, the eyeglass industry operated under a near monopoly that controlled the sales pipeline and price points. That these high prices would be passed on to consumers went unquestioned, even if that meant some people would go without glasses altogether. For another, people didn't really want to buy a product as carefully calibrated and individualized as glasses online. Besides, how could an online company even work? David and Neil would have to be able to offer stylish frames, a perfect fit, and various options for prescriptions.

With a $2,500 seed investment from Wharton's Venture Initiation Program, David and Neil launched their company in 2010 with a selection of styles, a low price of $95, and a hip marketing program. (They named the company Warby Parker after two characters in a Jack Kerouac novel.) Within a month, they'd sold out all their stock and had a 20,000-person waiting list. Within a year, they'd received serious funding. They kept perfecting their concept, offering an innovative home try-on program, a collection of boutique retail outlets, and an eye test app for distance vision. Today Warby Parker is valued at $1.75 billion, with 1,400 employees and 65 retail stores.

It's no surprise that Neil and David continued to use Warby Parker's success to deliver eyeglasses to those in need. The company's Buy a Pair, Give a Pair program is unique: instead of simply providing free eyeglasses, Warby Parker trains and equips entrepreneurs in developing countries to sell the glasses they're given. To date, 4 million pairs of glasses have been distributed through Warby Parker's program. This dual commitment to inexpensive eyewear for all, paired with a program to improve access to eyewear for the global poor, makes Warby Parker an exemplary assumption-busting social enterprise.

"It's not about the amount of wealth you can accumulate or the amount of profits you can drive, it's about the impact and change that you can create."

—NEIL BLUMENTHAL

Attorney Bryan Stevenson has been bursting through assumptions all his life, but his most ambitious effort has been his vow to end mass incarceration for those who suffer the legacy of racial inequality. As he says, "I believe each person in our society is more than the worst thing they've ever done." His Equal Justice Initiative has gone from its scrappy origins to winning major legal challenges eliminating excessive and unfair sentencing, exonerating innocent death row prisoners, confronting the abuse of the incarcerated and the mentally ill, and aiding children prosecuted as adults. "There is this burden in America that people of color bear," he explained in an interview with *Pacific Standard*. "This presumption of dangerousness weighs on you. And when we don't talk about it, when we don't name it, the burden only gets heavier. People of color have to navigate around these presumptions, and it is exhausting."

He knows something of that exhaustion. He entered first grade in Delaware in a segregated school before *Brown v. Board of Education* took effect, and although schools were integrated the following year, he was still not allowed to climb on the jungle gym during recess. Each time he went to the doctor's office, he and his parents entered through the back door.

Bryan saw firsthand that there was a divide that separated people in America, and he felt great empathy for those who failed because they never had a chance to bridge that gap. "An absence of compassion can corrupt the decency of a community, a state, a nation," he wrote in his powerful book *Just Mercy: A Story of Justice and Redemption*. "Fear and anger can make us vindictive and abusive, unjust and unfair, until we all suffer from the absence of mercy and we condemn ourselves as much as we victimize others. The closer we get to mass incarceration and extreme levels of punishment, the more I believe it's necessary to recognize that we all need mercy, we all need justice, and—perhaps—we all need some measure of unmerited grace."

Bryan has successfully argued several cases before the United States Supreme Court. In 2017, he won a historic ruling when the court deemed mandatory life-without-parole sentences for children seventeen or younger unconstitutional.

"The court took a significant step forward by recognizing the fundamental unfairness of mandatory death-in-prison sentences that don't allow sentencers to consider the unique status of children and their potential for change," said Bryan of the ruling. "The court has recognized that children need additional attention and protection in the criminal justice system." This is just mercy: challenging all of society to put aside our assumptions and allow true justice to prevail.

The most common trait that Big Bets share is that they often fly in the face of conventional wisdom, or defy belief before they are proven. And often the same is true of the people who make them—just like their big ideas they can often be underestimated. If you've ever heard, "It can't be done," then maybe you know you're onto something big! The stories in this chapter teach us that great ideas can come from anywhere and anyone, including those the world would sometimes count out. Can you stand in the face of disbelief in you or your idea and use the doubters as a source of motivation? Can you answer their doubts by saying, "Just watch me"?

FOUR

PEEK AROUND CORNERS

Invention isn't ruled by public opinion. "If I'd asked people what they wanted, they'd have said, 'Faster horses,'" Henry Ford famously said. The visionaries who create new realities must be able to peek around corners and see what others can't. When the automobile was introduced, people's minds turned immediately to the downsides of this new contraption—to the risks. It's always that way with new things. Think of the fears in our modern era about driverless cars. Many of history's most significant innovations have come from visionaries who had to then wait for the world to catch up.

When an advancement reaches mainstream acceptance, it is easy to lose sight of what life was like before. Who can imagine life without an Internet connection anymore? But as recently as 1995, only one in four families owned a computer! When America Online was founded in 1985, the country was far from being online. Only 3 percent of Americans were online at the time—and they were online an average of just one hour a week. Few jobs required computer skills, and no one walked around with smart devices in their pockets. I can recall with great clarity the number of times we heard, "Why would I ever need email?" or "My business doesn't need a connection to the Internet."

But we were on a mission to democratize access to ideas and information, so we presented a compelling offering to the world. And we persisted in our vision. It took us nine years to get the first million customers, but just seven *months* to get the second million. Today some people don't even use computers anymore; they use next-generation tablets or smartphones.

Peeking around corners involves either watching where the trends are headed or deciding to start a new one. Amazon is a singular example of this. At a time when people were nervous about putting credit card information online, Amazon got consumers so comfortable with online purchasing that people now allow companies to store their credit card information, track their purchases, and make personal recommendations for other items they might enjoy.

Amazon's founder, Jeff Bezos, has been a friend for many years, dating back to the earlier periods in technology when the company was a young start-up with a really Big Bet. In many ways, Jeff's life story is the embodiment of both the Be Fearless principles and the American Dream. Jeff was born to a seventeen-year-old mom who was still in high school. When Jeff was four years old his mom married a Cuban immigrant, and those of us who know Jeff have seen firsthand the incredible role both of his parents have played in his life. Growing up, Jeff spent summers with his grandparents on a ranch in Texas, where even as a small child he did chores; as he grew older, his work on the ranch began to shape his sense of resourcefulness and confidence. "We fixed windmills, and laid water pipelines, and built fences, and barns, and fixed the bulldozer," he said in an interview with *Business Insider*. He speaks of lessons taken from his experiences on the ranch, from the down-to-earth nature of problem solving to the importance of teamwork.

Jeff studied at Princeton and found success on Wall Street. He was a young hedge fund manager in 1994 when he told his parents about his idea to start an Internet company. His father's first question was, "What's the Internet?" But Jeff was captivated by the numbers. After reading that the Internet had grown 2,300 percent in one year, Jeff looked around for a product to launch, researching twenty different categories before settling on books. His parents were his first investors, handing over most of their savings. They weren't betting on the idea, Jeff said later, because they didn't understand the idea. They were betting on their son—even after he warned them that there was a 70 percent chance they'd lose their entire investment.

Jeff didn't know how his venture would turn out when he left his lucrative Wall Street career to jump into the emerging tech market. But as he later explained, "I knew when I was eighty that I would never, for example, think about why I walked away from my 1994 Wall Street bonus right in the middle of the year at the worst possible time. That kind of thing just isn't something you worry about when you're eighty years old. At the same time, I knew that I might sincerely regret not having participated in this thing called the Internet that I thought was going to be a revolutionizing event. When I thought about it that way . . . it was incredibly easy to make the decision." It was his Big Bet.

> *"There'll always be serendipity involved in discovery."*
> —JEFF BEZOS

It turned out he was on to something. Within a month, Amazon.com was doing $20,000 in sales. A year later, Jeff was able to raise $8 million in capital, and in 1997 the company went public. The following year, Amazon started selling music and videos, and soon other products too, including electronics, household goods, and toys.

As Amazon has grown into one of the most successful companies in America, Jeff's revolutionary model has generated some controversy. Economist Paul Krugman has claimed that Amazon "has too much power, and it uses that power in ways that hurt America"—a view shared by others who blame the company for declines in retail sales. But others would argue that Jeff didn't create this decline. He just recognized a trend and capitalized on it with a company that appealed to what consumers wanted: more choice, more convenience, and more competitive prices.

And Amazon has kept innovating, looking around corners to find new opportunities. When Jeff introduced the Kindle e-reader in 2007, there were hardly any ebooks—only 20,000 available for download. By the time the Kindle went on sale, Amazon had increased that to 90,000. Today there are more than 5 million ebooks available in Amazon's Kindle store, and millions more on other platforms. And Amazon has gone on to disrupt in other arenas with its video streaming service and smart devices like Alexa populating households everywhere.

Jeff Bezos's story is well known, but there are countless others peeking around corners to make Big Bets every day. One of my favorites is Sarah Parcak, a National Geographic Fellow and the 2016 winner of the $1 million TED Prize. It was her job title, Space Archaeologist, that first drew me to her work. Her Twitter handle—@IndyFromSpace—only added to my interest. Sarah is a vibrant woman whose enthusiasm for her field is infectious. She uses the very latest technology to find some of the oldest structures on the planet, uncovering hidden cultural treasures that lie beneath the surface of our earth—antiquities that time and natural elements have buried, such as pyramids and temples. Thanks to Sarah, archaeologists, who usually set out for a dig with limited data to guide them, can now be directed to "hot spots" where antiquities are most likely to be found.

Sarah credits her upbringing in Bangor, Maine, with providing the inspiration for her career. She recalls spending hours walking the beaches in search of sand dollars. "These shells are hard to find," she says. "They are covered in sand and difficult to see. Over time I got used to looking for them. I started seeing shapes and patterns that helped me to collect them." For Sarah, this digging developed into a skill for pattern recognition and grew into a passion for finding buried things. To date, her innovative use of satellite technology has led to the discovery of seventeen previously unknown pyramids.

But Sarah's dream doesn't stop there. Her wish that won her the TED Prize is to engage people everywhere as "citizen scientists" in identifying and protecting sacred cultural sites that are threatened by those out to exploit or destroy them, such as ISIS or antiquities traffickers. Standing on the TED stage, she declared: "Archaeologists are the cultural memory preservers and the cultural spokespeople for the billions of people and thousands of cultures that came before us. I believe that there are millions of undiscovered archaeological sites left to find. Discovering them will do nothing less than unlock the full potential of our existence."

The urgent need to identify and protect ancient sites around the world served to motivate Sarah to think big. Knowing there are millions of sites to be found, Sarah understood that even a Herculean effort by the two hundred or so space archaeologists wouldn't do much to impact the scale of the problem. Her big idea? Democratize archaeology and the search for ancient sites by creating and training a twenty-first-century army of global explorers. She would use her TED Prize money to build an online, crowdsourced, citizen scientist–based platform that would give citizens all over the world the chance to examine and identify hidden sites. This "big data" approach has served to unleash a global explorer revolution, with citizens exploring millions of small "tiles" or squares of territory photographed from space, identifying tens of thousands of potential ancient sites and features in multiple countries. Among the most prolific contributors is a woman in her nineties whose passion for archaeology was born when she and her husband dug up a fossil in their backyard in the 1950s—which goes to show that anyone from anywhere has something to contribute in helping to preserve cultural heritage worldwide.

As this chapter demonstrates, many Big Bets happen as a result of either watching where trends are headed or deciding to start a new one. And while there is no such thing as a crystal ball, many Big Bets were executed because someone boldly envisioned a different future—one not yet seen by others—and pursued it. What kind of world do you want to see? What kind of future do you want to build? The key is tuning out those who don't share your vision and persevering toward your goal.

FIVE

NOW GO, MAKE YOUR BIG BET

One day in high school I was walking with my headmaster, who'd asked what progress I'd made toward a certain goal. "I just can't seem to find the time to get it done," I said a bit sheepishly. He stopped, looked me in the eye, and replied, "You don't wait to *find* the time for what is important. You *make* the time for things that matter." It's a lesson I carry with me to this day, using my calendar to reflect what really matters.

Do you have a Big Bet for your personal or professional life? Decisions you make today can affect what happens down the road. The relationships you build, your professional affiliations, even how you spend your personal time all add up to a significant investment. So the question is, to what end? It's easy to get carried along without stopping to check if your path is leading you closer to your goals.

The Parkland high school students went to class one day, thinking about tests and graduation, only to be jolted from their ordinary lives by a mass shooting. They weren't ready—who can possibly be ready for something like that? But many of them took this tragedy as an opportunity to make desperately needed change.

Brian Chesky and Joe Gebbia had few resources to put behind any kind of bet, much less a big one. But when a problem needed solving, they built a solution from the ground up—literally, from an air mattress on the floor. Sara Blakely started with nothing but an idea and $5,000, but she had the tenacity to do the legwork (pardon the pun) that got Spanx in production. Jeff Bezos was watching trends, taking a cue from hockey great Wayne Gretzky, who spoke of watching "where the puck is going, not where it is."

How will *you* begin?

What would it mean for you to think futuristically, to refuse to accept life's presumed default positions? There are plenty of examples of people who have done just that, to great effect. Driverless cars seemed like science fiction when they were first proposed, but today they're on the horizon, as are drone delivery services. We can easily see a future without television sets and landlines. We can imagine clean water delivery systems, clean fuel technologies, and sources of food that have yet to be invented. Think about what that means for *you*, starting where you are. What yet-imagined future can you be a part of creating?

"The best way to predict the future is to create it." This quote is variously credited to Abraham Lincoln and management guru Peter Drucker. Whomever the source, the sentiment is a worthy one. Once you have a Big Bet, get to work. Define your objective, and then chunk it down into manageable parts. Every big idea starts with a first step forward. Then, when you know where you're headed, plant your flag. Consider how many audacious achievements can be tracked back to the moment a promise was made. When President Kennedy said, "We choose to go to the moon in this decade," the goal became real. I once spoke to an audience about JFK's moonshot promise, and an astronaut's wife in the room pointed out that when Kennedy talked about sending a man into space, he also said, "then return [him] safely to earth." That was a big part of Kennedy's bet too. What will be your moonshot? And how will you ground it in reality?

To make a Big Bet, steadily focus on your true north: the goals that propel you forward. For me, it has always been working to empower others. The true north will be your guiding light. It never changes. It's not about a job or any one endeavor. But it will always lead you where you need to go.

When I look at the changemakers featured in this section, I see people seeking a world that's different from ours in some significant way. For Barbara Van Dahlen, it's a place warriors can come home to support and safety. For Rachel Sumekh, it's one where no college student goes hungry. For Astro Teller, it's a world where technology can be harnessed to solve "impossible" problems. For the Parkland students, it's a world with communities where kids' lives matter more than guns. For Eunice Shriver, it's a world where having a disability can't stop you from winning.

What stands out to me most about many of these individuals is how they come from all walks of life. Many of them are everyday people like you and me—people whose most distinguishing feature is their passion for a dream they were determined to make come true.

PART TWO

BE BOLD, TAKE RISKS

Get uncomfortable

Embrace risk as R&D

Pick up where others left off

Risk or regret

Now go, find the "courage zone"

SIX

GET UNCOMFORTABLE

I steadied myself at the top of the telephone pole and looked down at the instructor thirty feet below. "I don't think I can do this," I shouted, with frustration and embarrassment. I had signed up for this adventure as part of an Outward Bound–type exercise. There were six of us in the group, and when the instructor had asked one of us to volunteer to go first, I'd raised my hand. Now I wasn't so sure.

The goal of the exercise was to climb thirty feet up to the top, and then walk another thirty feet across a pole laid out horizontally to the telephone pole on the opposite side. The adventure was called Out on a Limb, and that's exactly how I felt. I'd been standing at the top of the first pole for several minutes, my heart racing and my legs shaking, as my five teammates gaped up at me. Although I was secured in a harness, the thought of taking that first step onto the narrow horizontal pole had me frozen. "I really don't think I can do this," I said again, pushing back tears.

"But you can *try*," said the instructor, four words that would honestly change my life—or at least my perspective—in the years to come. *I could try.* If I failed or if I fell, so what? I was attached with a safety harness. But I didn't want to be the person who gave up and climbed down. I wanted to face my fear and own whatever the outcome would be.

So I took that first step out onto the pole, and then another, and another. Slowly, and with some wobbling, I proceeded along the pole. About a third of the way across I began to lose my balance. Just then I heard a voice from below: "You've got this! Stay focused! Keep going!" I stopped and steadied myself. Standing in midair with the nearest thing to cling to at least ten feet away, I took a deep breath and continued on across the pole. In some ways those steps—continuing on after a stumble—felt almost more challenging than the very first steps. I kept going, allowing myself only the briefest pause to touch the opposite pole before I turned around to retrace my steps. When my hands finally grasped the pole I had climbed, a cheer erupted from below. Everyone applauded and called out words of praise as I descended back to the ground.

With legs that were still shaking, I removed the harness and turned my attention to the remaining five who would follow in my footsteps. When we had all completed the exercise, we came together in a circle and talked about the experience.

At one point, the instructor eyed me with interest. "What was happening up there, Jean?" she asked. "What were you feeling?" I admitted that I'd felt scared. I thought I wouldn't be able to do it. Then she asked me a question no one had ever asked me before: "Do you think you have mostly chosen to pursue things you know you will be good at in life?" Whoa. I had never considered this; but upon reflection I realized that, yes indeed, I mostly had. My successes had typically come in areas where I had some degree of comfort and confidence. "Is there anything you've wanted to do but kept yourself from trying because you feared you wouldn't be good at it?" the instructor asked. I sat there for a long moment, considering. She suggested, "Why don't you make a list of things you've always thought about doing but resisted because of a fear you wouldn't excel."

When I returned to my room, I did make a list. It was fairly short, but I was still surprised to realize that I had grown so uncomfortable with risk. And while I didn't know it then, that list was the beginning of a new way of living—one that would bring me much more satisfaction and joy.

More than a decade after that day out on a limb, I experience a greater richness to life because I now deliberately take on endeavors that I'm not certain I can achieve. Yes, there have been disappointments, but they've been offset by my pride at not giving in to fear. It's been exhilarating to try such new things: mountain climbing, Tae Kwon Do, scuba diving with sharks, walking on sea ice in Antarctica. More vital than the physical risks, though, is the awareness, now infused through my life and work, that the moment I get comfortable is the moment I need to shift direction.

Perhaps there are fears holding you back from being bold or taking risks or simply trying something new. Like me, I hope you can find inspiration from the stories in the pages to come of people who took bold risks to achieve the extraordinary. These stories make clear that what separates fearless individuals from everyone else is not the absence of fear, but their ability to overcome it. President Jimmy Carter once said, "Go out on a limb. That's where the fruit is." Let these stories encourage you to embrace risk and enjoy the fruit of your new, bold efforts.

I have always been attracted to stories about great explorers, and becoming Chairman of the Board of Trustees of the National Geographic Society introduced me to so many new people who have put it all on the line to open the world for us all. I was particularly inspired by a woman named Eliza Scidmore, who had preceded me by more than a century as the first female board member of the National Geographic Society in 1892. I felt such a bond with Eliza. She too was a child of America's heartland, born in the Midwest in 1856. And Eliza's mother, like mine, wanted more for herself and for her children. Separated from her husband, she moved with her two children to Washington, DC, where she ran a boardinghouse. In the bustling capital, Eliza felt her world expand. She was surrounded by diplomats, politicians, and military leaders, many of them returned from travel to faraway places, who spoke of beauty and adventure. These stories instilled in Eliza a fascination with geography, and she spent long hours poring over maps. "Travel must have been born in me, like the original sin," she told an interviewer in 1890. "My daydreams were always of other countries."

In Eliza's time, any independent travel was difficult for a single woman, much less adventures to the uncharted places Eliza longed to visit. But she was determined, and so she found a very clever way of getting what she wanted. After graduating from Oberlin College at the age of nineteen, she began a career as a journalist, often going by the name E. R. Scidmore to disguise her gender. Soon "Mr." Scidmore became wildly popular, earning Eliza enough money to fund her journalistic pursuits. Her first great journey was as a passenger on a steamship to the wild frontiers of Alaska, where she chronicled the stories of the local tribes and the first white settlers, and wrote of the majesty of the unspoiled lands. In 1885, she published the first travel guide to the region, nearly seventy-five years before Alaska became the forty-ninth US state.

Accompanying her brother, who served in the US consulate in

Japan, Eliza traveled widely in the Far East, sending her impressions back home in vivid accounts. In 1890, she joined the newly founded National Geographic Society, becoming the first female writer and photographer for its magazine. Eliza's globe-trotting took her to India, China, Java (now Indonesia), Korea, Russia, and beyond, her contributions helping establish *National Geographic's* reputation for covering the nature and people of unknown places. She was an explorer at a time when a woman's place was "supposed" to be in the home.

It was on her first visit to Japan that Eliza saw what she would later call "the most beautiful thing in the world"—Japanese cherry blossom trees. She became convinced that these beautiful, delicate blooms could do much to add elegance to her own nation's capital and began to use her growing influence to champion the planting of Japanese cherry blossom trees around the "muddy and unattractive" Tidal Basin in Washington. It took her twenty years to see it happen, but she and First Lady Helen Taft pushed ahead with their plans. After officials from the US and Japan got wind of their ambitions, the idea caught on and gained momentum. In 1910, the first gift of two thousand trees was received from the Japanese government. Today these trees are synonymous with springtime in Washington, Eliza's perennial imprint on our world.

> *"It's your road, and yours alone. Others may walk it with you, but no one can walk it for you."*
> —RUMI

History is rich with stories of explorers we can use as models for our own ventures—like Sir Ernest Shackleton, whose leadership throughout his famous expedition to make the first transcontinental journey across Antarctica is legendary. When his ship was just a day's sail away from the continent, the pack ice floating in the frozen sea closed in around the *Endurance*, forbidding any movement. For months Shackleton and his men survived on the ship, using military-style discipline to keep order and divide the tasks that were necessary to keep them alive. When the *Endurance* was at last crushed by the ice, it happened slowly and with enough warning from the initial eerie creaking of the wood that Shackleton was able to rally his men and salvage lifeboats, which they dragged across the ice toward the open sea. Their plan: to journey hundreds of miles through one of the world's most hostile stretches of ocean.

Miraculously, the crew made it to Elephant Island, where a base camp was set up. But Shackleton knew that rescue would not likely come if the men remained, so with a crew of five he set out again in the small wooden boat through dangerous waters for South Georgia Island, hundreds of miles away. Upon reaching South Georgia Island, he faced a perilous climb over icy mountain ridges, but thoughts of his men awaiting rescue back on Elephant Island drove him on. At last, Shackleton came upon an outpost where he made arrangements for a rescue of his crew. All survived the harrowing adventure.

MBA leadership courses now study Shackleton's legacy, books and films tell his story, and generations of explorers have set out for fresh frontiers, inspired by the story of this truly fearless man. But in the years that followed his failed expedition, when asked about the extreme hardships he encountered, Shackleton would reply, "Difficulties are just things to overcome, after all."

In our modern era we can experience such moments of courage

in real time, not just as stories we read about. I've been lucky to have those chances. In 1981, I was privileged to be present at the launch of the first space shuttle, *Columbia*, at Kennedy Space Center in Florida. The congressional delegation from Florida had been invited to witness the launch, and my then-boss, Congressman E. Clay Shaw, generously invited me to come along. At the moment of the launch, there was an incredibly loud rumble, along with a distinct feeling that the very ground beneath my feet might give way. I felt it in my bones. Watching the sleek shuttle rise into the air, I was deeply conscious that it held the fates of living astronauts, whose personal courage was beyond anything I'd ever imagined. I remember thinking, "If they can do *this*, what can I do?"

Throughout my life, I've seen firsthand that the world is filled with people with great ambitions. I have listened to their doubts and seen the discomfort in their faces as they talk about stepping on untrodden ground. Often, those who use that discomfort to propel themselves forward are the ones who come out ahead. They may not make it on the first try. But often, like Shackleton or the astronauts I saw hurtling skyward, they keep going.

I was reminded of this on my first day in Antarctica on a trip with National Geographic in 2017, as I was coming down from an icy hike up a steep ridge. Feeling relieved that I had only slipped twice to no consequence, I spotted a curious chinstrap penguin making his way toward us. This penguin was surely an expert traveler on ice and snow, but he was so caught up in his observations that he lost his footing and fell on his tummy. Unfazed, he simply righted himself and proceeded on. Some of us chuckled. But the truth is, everyone can slip up, no matter our level of competence. The key is to get right back up and keep going.

If you are anything like me, getting uncomfortable is, well, *uncomfortable*. We would all prefer to live in the comfort zone of life, but as the stories in this chapter show, nothing extraordinary comes from the comfort zone. Risk taking requires boldness—stepping into unfamiliar territory and trying new, often unexpected things. The very nature of breakthroughs is that they have never been tried before. Are you considering a possible action that requires you to get uncomfortable and step out into unfamiliar territory? The hardest part is the first step forward. Like the advice I received when I was teetering thirty feet in the air on a telephone beam, just keep telling yourself, "But I can *try*."

SEVEN

EMBRACE RISK AS R&D

When I work with boards of traditional organizations, I can see the members squirm in their chairs if I ask a question about their appetite for risk taking. This happens even in organizations that are seeking to reinvent themselves. Few people are inclined to run *toward* risk. Instead, I often hear people ask, "How can we minimize or eliminate risk?"

But what if we substituted the term "research and development" for "risk taking"? When you change the image from a reckless act to an intentional, sometimes incremental process, the fear lessens. Rather than a matter of life or death, risk becomes part of the process of discovery.

Our brains are wired to avoid risk. In humanity's early days, physical danger was ever present, so our brains adapted to tell us when we needed to fight or run away. Today we need to help our brains go through a different exercise, asking ourselves: "What's the downside of the risk? What's the upside of the risk? What's the downside of doing nothing?"

Sometimes dipping a toe in the water is the best way to get comfortable with the idea of experimentation. In my work with more risk-averse organizations, I often suggest they think about making a limited investment, putting aside maybe only 1 percent of their budget for special projects to test out a new idea. In this way, risk stops being scary and becomes R&D.

Talk to private sector CEOs and they will be quick to point out that R&D is the lifeblood of innovative companies. Yes, some things will fail as you discover what works and what doesn't. But as Einstein reportedly said, "You never fail until you stop trying." This is true whether you're launching a program, developing a product, or starting a movement. I've often heard people from the social sector protest, "But we don't have funding for R&D!" My response is to remind them of the words of one of our greatest modern-day innovators, Steve Jobs: "Innovation has nothing to do with how many R&D dollars you have. When Apple came up with the Mac, IBM was spending at least one hundred times more on R&D. It's not about money. It's about the people you have, how you're led, and how much you get it." You don't need a big budget in order to experiment.

> *"You never fail until you stop trying."*
> —ALBERT EINSTEIN

Realistically, budgets are often stretched and funding for programs "locked." I see this especially with foundations or government programs, which can have rigid protocols. When nonprofits or governments experiment and fail, those failures are often labeled as waste or fraud or abuse, which discourages more risk taking.

Yet we all know about the value of experimenting early and often, because it's a common way of making breakthroughs in science and medicine. No credible scientific or medical institution exists without a lab—a dedicated space where experimentation can take place. The same thinking can easily be applied to efforts led by individuals and nonprofits. No matter the sector, everyone should also feel empowered to experiment and test different ideas, market opportunities, or even twists on their business models.

Science and medicine also offer spectacular examples of outsized risks that have changed the world. Consider smallpox. In the late 1700s, when smallpox was ravaging villages, with a death rate as high as 35 percent, Dr. Edward Jenner observed that milkmaids who previously had suffered from cowpox did not later catch smallpox, even when exposed to the disease. So Jenner experimented with what seemed like a crazy idea at the time—injecting a small amount of cowpox into healthy individuals to test whether it could protect them from contracting smallpox. Today, more than two hundred years later, vaccines are commonly deployed against a great many diseases, and the vaccine Jenner discovered led to the eradication of smallpox around the world.

Another great example of this is the work of National Geographic explorer Jane Goodall. I still treasure the memory of the first time I met her. She had come "home" to National Geographic as part of the annual Explorers Symposium. As she gracefully took the stage and spoke of her important work in an unforgettable British cadence, the audience sat mesmerized. Indeed, long before the 2017 hit movie *Jane* that chronicled her important work in Africa, she was well known to the world. It was in 1965 that National Geographic produced a film about her and her work in the Gombe Stream National Park in Tanzania entitled *Miss Goodall and the Wild Chimpanzees*. And photographs of Jane's early work in the field with chimpanzees are considered by many to be among the most iconic National Geographic images.

Jane's life has been a model of fearlessness. It was her love of animals and her interest in working with them that first took her to visit a friend in Africa when she was twenty-six. At the time, the famous paleoanthropologist Louis Leakey was doing groundbreaking work on early human origins, and Jane boldly asked to see him. Upon meeting her, Leakey hired her as a secretary on the spot. She had no college degree, but he planned to mentor her. Within months, Leakey, who was married and thirty years Jane's senior, told her he was in love with her. She has spoken of being horrified by this development and very worried that her constant rebuffing of his advances would spell trouble for her future in the scientific work she had dreamed of. But, despite her lack of interest in him, Leakey continued to be her champion, and he raised the necessary funds to enable her field work with chimpanzees.

Since Jane had not been schooled in traditional protocols of animal behavior observations and research, she developed her own unconventional methods for observation of the chimpanzees. Over time, she assigned the chimps personal names and carried sketchbooks to make notes and drawings of their behaviors. Soon the chimps routinely came to visit and began to interact with her in the field. Jane's research led to dramatic breakthroughs. Her observation that chimps weren't just using tools but making them out of found objects challenged conventional wisdom that only humans were capable of such complexities. Leakey, for one, was inspired to send a telegram that read, "Now we must redefine 'tool,' redefine 'man,' or accept chimpanzees as human."

Later Jane received a PhD from Cambridge University. Her

work in the field has spanned fifty-five years of research, and she is widely recognized today as the foremost expert on chimpanzees. She formed the Jane Goodall Institute in 1977 and has won recognition and accolades from around the world, including being named a UN Messenger of Peace in 2002 for her life's work.

Jane's story reminds us that sometimes approaching the unknown without a traditional set of research protocols or expected outcomes can produce remarkable results. Jane was successful and saw things that other scientists didn't because she did not have bias or preconceived notions about the world of chimpanzees. This enabled her to be bold, build her own method of R&D, and change the world in the process. It was a huge risk to travel to Africa, to go into the field without proper training, and to publish findings that were contrary to the scientific understanding of her day. She was undaunted and fearless, and embraced the idea of risk as necessary R&D. In 2017, when Jane came back to National Geographic and we proudly gathered for the premiere of the *Jane* film, I looked on with some awe as she greeted each guest patiently and graciously. I was struck anew by her powerful inspiration, and by the extraordinary contributions she has made to her field and to the world.

• • •

Jonas Salk took a big risk too. In 1947, while in his early thirties, he became director of the Virus Research Laboratory at the University of Pittsburgh, where he was charged with developing new tools to fight polio, a life-threatening disease that resulted in half a million cases of paralysis or death each year. Salk's work is of special significance to me since I had a close family member who contracted polio in his twenties. My dad's brother, a tall, strong, and handsome young man, came home from World War II with dreams of the life he wanted to build. When polio struck shortly after his return to the States, it paralyzed him and he spent the rest of his life in a wheelchair.

At the time my uncle contracted polio, scientists believed that vaccines needed to contain some kind of "active" virus to be effective. Salk wanted to experiment with a vaccine that contained an "inactive" virus, hoping that this approach would generate the much-needed protective antibodies in those he vaccinated without putting them at risk for developing the disease. He so believed in the safety of his vaccine that he administered it first to himself, his wife, and their children. Today, thanks to the contributions of Jonas Salk, there are very few cases of polio reported anywhere in the world. Like Jenner before him, Salk's commitment to experimenting early and often has saved tens of millions of lives.

The good news is that the lab approach isn't just reserved for scientists. Because of advances in technology, the process of testing and validating new ideas can be streamlined, limiting the risk up front. Testing a plan or product quickly and with limited resources isn't a new idea; focus groups are commonly employed to determine a product's appeal, and beta tests have been used for decades. What's different today is that it's possible to put your concept in front of the market and start absorbing market signals before there is a real product, and in some cases before a company or organization is even formed. This, in turn, creates a new egalitarian landscape that spreads the opportunity.

In his celebrated book *The Lean Startup*, Eric Ries calls this early prototyping process "build, measure, learn," and he promotes the idea of doing so with a "minimum viable product," or MVP—

that is, using the least amount of time and effort required to establish the viability of a product, service, or idea. Rather than testing a product repeatedly until it's perfect, Ries and the companies that have employed this strategy push out new products as soon as they're workable, typically to a small subset of loyal customers, and then gather feedback about how to improve them.

To make this point, Ries highlights the story of Zappos, the highly successful online shoe seller. When Zappos founder Nick Swinmurn had the idea for the company, people told him that buying shoes online was crazy, because you have to try them on. But Swinmurn wasn't convinced. He went to retailers and asked if he could take pictures of their shoes and put them online. Then he built a one-page site with the pictures and included a way for people to order them. When somebody ordered shoes, Swinmurn would go buy them and ship them off. He obviously couldn't do this for long, but he did it long enough to learn where the challenges would be and what customers wanted. Then he launched his company. There are many examples like Zappos of building improvement measures into the design process and inviting customers to take part in innovation. In this way, risk becomes R&D, and opportunities flourish.

The stories and underlying data in this chapter highlight a mind shift, from thinking of risk as a big, scary leap, to seeing it as essential to advancing an idea or initiative. We no longer can afford to stand still in a fast-changing world filled with so many needs. Each of us should embrace the concept of constantly trying new things and figuring out different ways to solve old problems. In the process, let's shift our minds to recognize that the risks we take represent our own version of necessary R&D—part of the process toward great achievement.

I'm not sure why research and development isn't something we are all encouraged to build into our lives. Long before the pursuit of a Big Bet, R&D can play a role in helping us avoid stagnation by constantly calling us to go back to the drawing board. And as this chapter makes clear, it doesn't require a big budget or a physical lab. The key is the willingness to commit time and energy to the process. Can you identify a few things to test to advance your big idea to the next stage?

EIGHT

PICK UP WHERE OTHERS LEFT OFF

So much of my lifelong learning has come from books. I use the wisdom gleaned from many of them in my work. A few years ago I read a book that so resonated with our work at the Case Foundation that we made a vow to read it together as a team. Then, with the benefit of after-work wine and cheese, we gathered to share our reflections and to discuss how we might apply the book's lessons to our own work in the days ahead. It was a transformative moment that we all vividly recall. That book was *How We Got to Now* by Steven Johnson. In it, he sets out to dispel the myth that innovation requires an individual genius with an "aha!" moment, as we referenced earlier. Johnson writes: "Big ideas coalesce out of smaller, incremental breakthroughs." He goes on to tell the story of Thomas Edison, a man we so associate with genius that we often refer to the "aha!" moment as the "lightbulb" moment. But Johnson makes it clear that it wasn't that simple. Edison wasn't even first. Early patents on the lightbulb preceded Edison's by the better part of a century, and dozens of others received patents for portions of the invention we credit Edison with today. What Edison was good at was being a fast and effective follower—taking nascent ideas that had already been tested and bundling them with new insights and a fresh team.

Johnson's point about Edison is this: he didn't just invent technology, he invented an entire system for inventing. Edison himself understood that innovation and iterative development often go hand in hand, openly acknowledging that he borrowed from the work of others. "I am quite correctly described as more of a sponge than an inventor," he said. It is the wise entrepreneur who understands this. And if you look at the team systems used at Bell Labs, Xerox, and some of the later classic innovation labs, you'll see they took Edison's approach and applied it.

Perhaps I have a special appreciation for picking up where others left off because I spent my early career helping to build digital online services—the companies that gave many of us our first experience of the Internet. I started with the nation's first pure play online service, The Source—a text-based information utility for consumers that featured early versions of email, conferencing, and content ranging from an encyclopedia to stock quotes. The fatal flaws that would limit scale and mainstream acceptance weren't so obvious back then. For example, these exciting services came across the telecommunications wire at the speed of 300 baud. What's 300 baud? The equivalent of 300 bits of data passing per second. Content today comes across at 100 million bits per second. So it was S-L-O-W. How slow? It would have taken forty hours to download the average song back then. And it was expensive. Accessing the services required a $100 subscription fee and hourly charges that ranged from $7 to $20, depending on the time of day.

Still, underlying this slow, expensive service was a really powerful idea, democratizing access to information and communication.

And it was that *idea*—never mind the kinks—that attracted followers. These services had the potential to level the playing field in a way that could change the way people lived, worked, and played. But some iteration was needed.

I landed at one more (failed) online service before I found myself at a start-up that would introduce something new to the world. Led by a founding team of three—Steve Case, Marc Seriff, and Jim Kimsey—this start-up set to work picking up where others left off. Steve, who would become CEO of AOL, was brilliant at understanding the shortcomings of the other young companies around us, and he led the team to experiment in areas that had previously limited growth for our competitors. This included consumer-friendly pricing, appealing graphic interfaces, and a "membership" approach that encouraged engagement, feedback, and a sense of community. And it worked. After early struggles, we hit a tipping point and people jumped on—a *lot* more people. At its peak, AOL had nearly 30 million subscribers, and was the first Internet company to go public.

But the story of AOL cannot be told without understanding how it benefited from the developments and failures of the services that came before. Steve wisely led AOL to be a good "sponge"— paying attention to market signals and evolving constantly to improve our offerings. And while AOL ushered in many exciting innovations, it also benefited greatly from what Steven Johnson refers to as "smaller, incremental breakthroughs."

Facebook, Google, and Twitter, in turn, all benefited from the innovations that AOL introduced. The founders of each of these companies have spoken about AOL as an early influence; for example, Mark Zuckerberg "hacked" AOL Instant Messenger in high school. These businesses represent a piece of what AOL brought to the world. Facebook looks a little like a next-generation version of AOL Member Pages, Twitter like AOL's instant messaging, and Google like a significant leap forward from AOL's early content search engines. Innovators can take major leaps or make a Big Bet by looking at where previous efforts fell short, and fully exploiting the lessons of those failures.

There is a catalytic power to bold endeavors; their impact is multiplied by the effect they have on others. The micro-lending movement was first pioneered by Muhammad Yunus, winning him a Nobel Prize. Jessica Jackley remembers being in the audience as a young woman when she heard him speak, describing the power of micro-lending to help smart, hardworking entrepreneurs across the globe—entrepreneurs who also happened to be poor. Jessica was so excited by the prospect of putting her own twist on this idea that she quit her job and moved to Africa to launch Kiva. She didn't have much to work with at first—just a digital camera and a website. But she and her Kiva cofounder, Matt Flannery, started from there, sending stories and pictures of people needing small loans to friends and family back home. By the end of the first year, their company had lent $500,000 in small amounts. And while there have been peaks and valleys in the dozen years since, today more than 2.5 million borrowers from eighty-three countries have received more than $1 billion in loans. The loans can be as small as $25, and projects are crowdfunded, so that each loan involves multiple lenders. And remember, these are not donations; the re-payment rate is 97 percent. Those who participate can see their small contributions spark a movement across the globe—such as a fabric business by a former child bride in India, funded with a

$570 loan, which employs two people plus her husband; and a thriving goat farm on the West Bank, crowdfunded with $2,000 by sixty-nine lenders.

I am struck by the way Jessica refused to be intimidated by what she didn't know and didn't have. At first, she only knew she could do one thing—tell stories and take pictures. But in time she was able to achieve the same global impact as a large philanthropic organization—not with charity, but with a hand up. The recipients of micro-loans, themselves models for starting right where you are, also have an impact far beyond their small companies. They show others in their communities what is possible.

Microbusinesses aren't just creating opportunity in under-developed countries. Many note that they're also having a positive impact across America. Not only do microbusinesses provide the extra income that helps people escape poverty, but they bring valuable products and services into underserved communities. They can help revitalize struggling Main Streets. From That's a Wrap!, a gift-wrapping store in Atlanta, to BBQ Rowe, a catering company in Tennessee, to Mama Coo's Boutique, a vintage shop in Detroit, everyone can start an all-American enterprise, with ingenuity, guts, and a little help from anyone willing to provide a small loan.

• • •

It's in my husband's nature to continue to try new stuff. Today Steve is taking forward an initiative called Rise of the Rest, which funds entrepreneurs across America. Riding a bus between the coasts to places that are often ignored by investors, but where the vast majority of Fortune 500 companies have been founded, and bringing press and investors along, he spends a week in these towns spotlighting the talent, innovation, and opportunities that exist there. I think in part Steve was inspired by our "Getting America Online" tour back in our AOL days, which crossed America looking for those who saw the future and wanted to get "on board." In each city he visits, Steve finds those looking to make a Big Bet, take a risk, and help new companies thrive. People like you and me who have decided that the time is right to Be Fearless. Towns across America's heartland are beginning to coalesce around entrepreneurs with new ideas, and investors are waking up too, realizing more and more the great talent and exciting new businesses that are dotting the whole of this country's landscape.

Innovation is needed everywhere, and it's happening not just in urban centers but in rural communities as well. For example, Justin Knopf, a young fifth-generation farmer, is calling on farmers to reject some of the conventional wisdom that has dominated farming for hundreds of years in hopes of saving one of our planet's most precious resources: soil. As Miriam Horn explains in *Rancher, Farmer, Fisherman*, Justin's attachment to his family farm runs deep. His ancestors came to Kansas as homesteaders and have farmed the same land for 160 years. In the Knopf family, memories of the Dust Bowl that blew away billions of tons of topsoil from farms across Kansas in the 1930s are not easily forgotten. Although not commonly understood, soil erosion remains a challenge for farmers today, and represents a grave threat to the planet's future. More than a third of all the earth's organisms live in soil, sustaining precious photosynthesis that helps provide us with food and oxygen. When soil is disturbed, the result is a dangerous release of carbon into the earth's atmosphere.

Science wasn't necessarily an interest in Justin's early years, but he was involved in farmwork and came to understand the impacts of severe drought, dangerous storms, and extreme heat. When he was fourteen, Justin's dad gave him a piece of his own land to oversee, and Justin experienced firsthand the struggles of farmland versus nature—soil that washed away, weeds growing out of control, and depressing crop yields.

But Justin's love of the land never wavered. After high school, he headed to Kansas State University, where he was exposed to a radical new concept by one of his professors: the preservation of soil microbes. The professor encouraged his students to adapt their farming methods to focus on preserving soils. At about the same time, Justin learned of a farmer near the hometown of a college friend who was preventing losses from both soil and water. Justin's interest was piqued. He and his friend loaded up a van and drove across Kansas into Nebraska, where Justin had what he later called "a dawning moment." The technique they witnessed in Nebraska was called "no tilling," using machines that enabled planting without tilling the fields, leaving the soil's rich biodiversity mostly undisturbed. No-till farming also involved rotating crops to build up the nutrients in the soil and limit infestations.

Justin couldn't believe what he was seeing. He excitedly shared news of these techniques with his father and brother and designed a plan to begin testing the new approach in a limited number of fields. They agreed to start with a small fourteen-acre plot, and based on the results scale from there. Only a few years later, Justin was seeing triple the yields from his fields using this new technique, and soon more and more of the farm's 4,500 acres were cultivated using the no-till process.

Since those early days, Justin has become recognized as a leader in the no-till farming movement, spreading his knowledge to help others learn sustainable practices to conserve soils while increasing yields. His passion for protecting earth's precious resources has taken him to Washington, DC, to advise on policy and turned him into an outspoken champion of what is today an expanding movement.

Justin's story reminds us that there is always room for new thinking, even in some of the most traditional sectors. But it also speaks to the value of measured versus "bet the farm" reckless risk, when taking new ideas forward. Justin hopes to usher in a new agricultural era to meet the demands of an ever more crowded world.

It's striking how often bold endeavors spring from problems that hit home. Consider Alexander Graham Bell (who, incidentally, was president of the National Geographic Society in its early years). His mother lost her hearing when he was twelve, and he spent his young years finding different techniques to communicate with her. His focus on sound technology and communications stemmed from his personal struggle and he turned his passion into a career helping the hearing impaired as a renowned teacher of the deaf in Boston, all the while developing innovations to help this community communicate. Many believe it was his marriage to one of his students, Mabel Hubbard, a young woman who had lost her hearing at age five, that reinforced his connection to this field and anchored his commercial work. Few developments have so changed the world as Alexander Graham Bell's telephone, but what's often lost in the telling of that story is that it all started with a problem Bell was trying to solve.

NINE

RISK OR REGRET

In the 1980s, when I was a marketing manager at GE, I thought my career was on a good path. GE's management development training was world renowned, and I was lucky to be chosen for it—it usually indicated a bright future. Then I got a call. A start-up down the road was interested in talking to me about coming in to head up its marketing efforts. The product I was working on at GE was an early online service, known as GEnie. It's why I was at GE in the first place. I'd come to the company convinced that the power and impressive budgets of such a well-respected brand would get more people online, allowing GEnie to dominate the market. Once settled in my role, however, I began to see things differently. GE's dominance in other markets limited its appetite to take big risks in this new, emerging field. The large marketing budgets I had been promised came with unexpected strings. The budgets for the company's established products and services were determined based on the revenue they brought in. GEnie was a new product, so all my department had was a belief that investments in GEnie would yield future revenues. This wasn't selling well at headquarters. The powers that be wanted to focus on sure things, not pie-in-the-sky dreams.

Suddenly the idea of jumping to a start-up that had just raised a new round of capital seemed like a surer path to building a more connected world. But I was taken aback by the reaction of those closest to me. "Leave your job at GE? Are you crazy?" they would ask, sometimes shrilly. "You have no idea if this new company will even survive. Why would you put everything at risk?" I began to doubt myself. But it was the risk of *not* taking the risk that caused me to make the leap. I joined the company that would become AOL and helped build a service that helped usher in the Internet revolution, and changed countless lives.

Looking back, I wouldn't trade that experience for the world. But in those earliest days, as we tried to attract more talent to our start-up, we came across people who were unwilling to risk a good thing for the possibility of an extraordinary thing. Those who passed up the opportunity to have a ride on our rocket ship often share with me their feelings of regret to this day.

The importance of taking risks isn't just a business calculation. It's a *life* calculation. For example, it's a crucial factor in parenting. There is a growing body of research that recognizes the importance of allowing children to take risks as an important part of healthy development. I struggled with that as a mom when my kids were young. Since my first instinct was to be protective, it wasn't always comfortable to let my children take risks. The irony was that I clearly recognized that the risks I was allowed to take as a child helped build resilience and independence. Sometimes it takes the influence of others—partners, friends, extended family members, etc.—who can bring a different perspective to help find the right balance. And even keeping up with important research on the subject can embolden a parent to embrace reasonable risk taking in the lives of children. *Psychology Today* published an article entitled "Risky Play: Why Children Love It and Need It," by Dr. Peter Gray, who had this to say: "We deprive children of free, risky play, ostensibly to protect them from danger, but in the process we set them up for mental breakdowns. Children are designed by nature to teach themselves emotional resilience by playing in risky, emotion-inducing ways. In the long run, we endanger them far more by preventing such play than by allowing it. And, we deprive them of fun."

• • •

It can be easy to get caught up in protecting the status quo, or what seems comfortable, rather than pursuing a different path. And yet, as Josh Linkner says in his book *The Road to Reinvention*, "It turns out that playing it safe has become recklessly dangerous."

> *"It turns out that playing it safe has become recklessly dangerous."*
> —JOSH LINKNER

Consider the cautionary tale of Kodak. Kodak's story starts with its founding by George Eastman in 1888. With photography still a relatively young art, Eastman saw an opportunity to democratize it, taking photography beyond its then-limited use in professional studios out to the consumer. In 1900, Kodak introduced an easy-to-use, lightweight camera for amateurs, known as the Brownie, which sold for one dollar. For Kodak, it was the film used in the camera, then sold for just fifteen cents, that provided the recurring profits that enabled the company to continue to grow and innovate. Kodak became so synonymous with photography that the phrase "It's a Kodak moment" came to describe memorable moments in life.

Then, in the 1970s, a Kodak engineer, Steve Sasson, and the company's chief technician, Jim Schueckler, tested a new technology that could produce a photographic image on a screen without the use of film. Such experimentation at a company sustained by the sale of film was fearless in its own right. Kodak had billions of dollars in sales and boasted a 70 percent market share in film. Could it risk throwing its weight into a new arena that might undermine its core business? In the end, Kodak couldn't make the shift. Concerned about protecting its lucrative film business, the company was slow to embrace this revolutionary form of digital imaging and failed to invest adequately in it, leaving the door open for competitors to step in. And step in they did. A Japanese competitor, Fujifilm, gobbled up Kodak's market share in traditional film, offering a lower-priced product to consumers. Meanwhile, the digital market was exploding—by 2003, digital cameras outsold film cameras, and Kodak faced disruption across its product lines. In 2012, the company filed for Chapter 11 bankruptcy. The same company that democratized photography in the nineteenth century refused to take the risk of riding the next leap into the twenty-first.

Kodak's opposite would be a company like Netflix, which has gone through several iterations, totally changing its business model to stay on top of trends. In the beginning, cofounders Reed Hastings and Marc Randolph had a simple premise: a customer-friendly rental company that would deliver movies right to your door. Hastings was still smarting from paying forty dollars after losing a video store's cassette for *Apollo 13* when he had the idea of charging customers a monthly rental fee, and having them send back their previous rentals to order new titles. By being a good sponge and watching the shortcomings of other offerings, Netflix created a compelling consumer experience. Convenience, check. Quick delivery, check. Inexpensive, check. Easy returns, check. No late fees, check. Large title library, check. Netflix was so successful that it killed the brick-and-mortar movie rental model; large companies like Blockbuster folded.

But the Netflix team refused to rest on its laurels, building a new video streaming service to both fend off competitors and maintain its leadership in the video delivery business. The transition was not as smooth as Reed Hastings would have liked, including a now-famous apology to customers when changes in the pricing structure alienated many of its original DVD customers. However, by making a bold leap into streaming, Netflix continued to innovate, refusing to play it safe. By 2013 the company had more customers than ever before. It was a big, risky pivot—and it paid off.

Netflix could have continued as a successful video streaming service, but it decided to take another leap that many people thought was crazy, into developing original programming. Again, there were predictions of doom. How could a streaming service hope to compete with networks, or with HBO and Showtime? The key was high-quality programming, beginning with *House of Cards* and *Orange Is the New Black*. Netflix became equated with top-quality original movies and TV, and did so well that other companies, such as Amazon, followed suit. There is little doubt that when the original programming market becomes saturated or no longer plays to Netflix's advantage, Reed Hastings will explore pivoting again.

Another quintessential pivot story also comes to mind. It wasn't so long ago that a podcasting platform called Odeo was introduced to the world. Thanks to a solid track record and business plan, the founders of Odeo were successful in attracting early capital. But as they began building their customer base, Apple announced it would include podcasts in its well-established iTunes platform, pushing Odeo out of the market.

Almost overnight, Odeo, led by CEO Evan Williams, realized it had to find another application for its platform. It created an employee challenge, and three now-legendary members of the team—Jack Dorsey, Biz Stone, and Noah Glass—came up with the concept of micro-messaging: short blogging updates comprising 140 characters that could be sent to one's friends or "followers" on the platform. Odeo redefined its mission: to give everyone the power to create and share ideas and information instantly. That quick pivot created the company we know today as Twitter.

And what of those who don't take risks? Sony Pictures will long lament its 1998 failure to do a deal that would have given it the film rights to Marvel's stable of superheroes. When the studio first approached Marvel Entertainment, a struggling comic book company, for the rights to Spider-Man, Marvel offered to sell Sony movie rights to all of its unlicensed characters, including Iron Man, Thor, and Black Panther, for $25 million. No, Sony responded, it only wanted Spider-Man. It was unwilling to take a risk on fringe characters. Marvel sold Sony only the rights to Spider-Man for $10 million and 5 percent of gross profits.

Sony set Marvel on the unlikely course of becoming a successful film studio—so successful that it was purchased by Disney in 2009 for over $4 billion. For Marvel knew what Sony could not grasp and would not risk: that there was an appetite for a range of characters. The Marvel blockbuster *Black Panther* was not only a financial hit but also, with its nearly all-black cast, a cultural phenomenon. Within a month of its release, it had earned $1 billion worldwide, and it is now the third-highest-grossing movie of all time in the United States.

There was a big player behind the scenes in this drama—the Walt Disney Company. Disney was smart enough to acquire Marvel just as it was beginning to thrive, and for the last decade, under the leadership of CEO Bob Iger, Disney has undergone its own radical reinvention to stay ahead of the times. Iger has faced threats from all sides—not the least being the growth of streaming services—with an eye to the future more than to the past. He recognizes that the Disney "brand," so iconically built and cultivated by Walt Disney, needs to keep pace in a market that has changed rapidly. Sentimentality can lead to paralysis and narrow thinking. Iger is determined to not let that happen to Disney.

> *"If you want to thrive in a disrupted world, you have to be incredibly adept at not standing still."*
> —BOB IGER

Even individuals often are unwilling to put at risk what they have achieved. It's not surprising that so many breakthroughs come out of desperate situations, where there is little to lose. The more we rack up success, the less willing we often are to put it on the line.

Having said that, of course people and organizations vary in their willingness to try new things, so it's important to measure your capacity for risk. The annals of history are replete with ideas and companies that had great ideas that failed and have now been forgotten. And for every AOL, there are lots of examples of companies and ideas that went the way of The Source and GEnie, two online efforts that didn't break through. Once you know your risk tolerance, you can begin to build a framework that either adheres to it, limits it, or seeks to stretch it. Start by knowing who you are. Then find your courage.

For many people, regrets in life often aren't tied to things they have done, but rather to those things they wished they had done but simply did not. Is there a Big Bet or bold endeavor that calls to you but you've convinced yourself can't be done? The stories in this chapter demonstrate the power of seizing the moment, and highlight the regret that comes from choosing a more comfortable path or tuning out the voice calling you to something transformative. When you consider getting out of your comfort zone and trying something new to advance your Big Bet, make a point of writing down the downside of *not* taking the risk.

TEN

NOW GO, FIND THE "COURAGE ZONE"

Here's the reality: greatness doesn't come from the comfort zone. That's true both personally and professionally. The "courage zone" is often where we see really exciting things happen. You might take a measured risk, or experiment until you get it right. But whatever your process, embarking on an experiment whose outcome you can't predict takes courage.

In her book *Stop Playing Safe*, author Margie Warrell introduces the concept of moving from a mind-set of *fear* to one of *courage*. She writes that the process starts with a basic challenge: "Know your why." That is to say, the courage to pursue bold actions comes when you're in tune with yourself and what matters to you. Warrell notes that studies done around the world show that up to 50 percent of the global workforce don't believe that what they do matters. You can't achieve great things if you don't pursue what matters to you.

In a goal-centric world, it's easy to think of success as the point where you feel comfortable. For many people, getting established in a chosen career is grueling. During periods of struggle, one can easily linger on the vision of a time when worries cease. But if you're trying to make a bold change in the world, you have to keep pushing forward.

It's this constant quest that distinguishes you. But that doesn't mean you have to jump off the next cliff you see. Start by being a good observer. Take note when you witness a bold action. And take small bold actions yourself every day. When you do one small thing you didn't think you could, it strengthens you for the next.

Experiments are happening all around us. But in this fast-paced world, we can't always wait for a thirty-year study and a double-blind test group. We can't wait for the perfect set of circumstances—as we're finishing one experiment, we need to be thinking about the next. And when we think a certain intervention is working, we have to take a peek down the road to see what new dynamics could challenge our assumptions or provide an even better solution. It's this type of thinking that has kept companies like Apple ahead, while less nimble and often bigger players have fallen behind. It's the scariest thing in the world to change your business plan, or your life plan, in midstream, but who among us would rather be Blockbuster than Netflix?

> *"You must do the thing you think you cannot do."*
> —ELEANOR ROOSEVELT

Having said that, boldness isn't recklessness. Take a lesson from companies like Zappos, and be bold one step at a time. Advance steadily. Let iteration be your friend. Progress often means borrowing the lessons and perfecting what has come before with a bigger, better bet.

If there's a problem you're burning to address—whether with

a new business, a new product, or a new social enterprise—before you do anything else, educate yourself about who has done what to attempt to solve that problem. Learning what iterative steps have already been taken can save you precious time and money. Look at successes, look at failures. Remember, it doesn't take a genius to accomplish something great. Just be a good sponge and go from there.

The truth is, I was uncomfortable with risk for most of my life. I still struggle with being fearless. But what I *can* do is find the discipline to face down my fear and take those first steps forward. My guess is that you can too.

PART THREE

MAKE FAILURE MATTER

Crash and learn

Fail in the footsteps of giants

Beat the odds

Take the long view

Now go, learn from failure

ELEVEN

CRASH AND LEARN

My heart still skips a beat or two when I talk about my own fail-ures. I'm not being glib. It's easy to fall into self-doubt, recrimina-tion, and even despair. Everyone has felt these emotions at some point in life's journey—everyone! It's what happens next that de-fines what we make of the experience. While not all failures have a happy ending, most happy endings have a failure story.

If you examine the life of anyone who has achieved something extraordinary, you'll find a story of failure somewhere along the way. Sometimes you really have to look for it, because too often as people advance through life they sanitize their stories, making it sound as if everything was carefully planned. But we do a disservice to others—especially to young people—if we aren't honest about our failures. When I spend time on college campuses, I go out of my way to talk about my own "failure résumé," recounting what didn't go so right on my career journey, including some pretty epic failures. I usually do this after receiving a glowing introduction, and as I recount my failures, I see at first looks of disbelief in the audience. As I continue, however, I begin to see another emotion on the students' faces—relief at the realization that you can fail forward to something better, or, as I like to quote from the Japanese proverb: "Fall down seven times; get up eight."

> *"Only those who dare to fail greatly can ever achieve greatly."*
> —ROBERT F. KENNEDY

We all face personal failures, whether in marriage, in relationships, in social situations, or by letting others down. I certainly have. These are painful. However, failures in our professional lives are often much more public. I know this from experience. As I faced one of the most difficult failures of my career, I knew that I had a choice to make: I could try to sweep it under the rug, sugarcoat it, or come clean.

The program in question, PlayPumps, was one of the most ambitious and exciting initiatives launched at the Case Foundation. Our goal was to bring clean drinking water to ten sub-Saharan countries and hundreds of villages. We loved the technology—a way to generate clean water by using children's merry-go-rounds to pump the water. Think of the merry-go-round as a windmill on its side. We knew people need clean water, and that children love to play. It seemed like a win-win.

When we were first introduced to the technology and saw the business model for its deployment, we believed it had enormous potential. We jumped in to help create PlayPumps International–US as a fund-raising and marketing organization to support the initiative. We launched the effort with great fanfare at the 2006 Clinton Global Initiative, with First Lady Laura Bush on one side of me and former President Bill Clinton on the other. Also onstage with me were my husband, Steve, and fellow philanthropist Ray Chambers (now the UN Secretary General's Special Envoy for Health).

There was a lot of early excitement about this new technology. Dozens of partners joined us in supporting the effort. There were some hiccups in the early years, but we patiently worked with partners on the ground to get things right, and we felt good about the progress.

But as the years passed, questions continued to pop up, and we realized that the program wasn't meeting the high standards required. Our team spent a year trying to address some of the shortcomings being reported in the field so we could get the initiative back on track. We came to realize that we couldn't assure the scale or quality of the program on the ground. We had a hard choice to make, with three options. One was to stubbornly continue on a path that growing evidence suggested was unwise. A second was to pull the plug and invest the time and capital elsewhere. And the third option was to take a step back, regroup, and attempt to go forward in a new and more effective way. We decided that the third option was the right way to go. After all, our belief that clean water is one of the great causes of our time hadn't changed. But we had to acknowledge that there were likely better ways to advance this cause. In May 2009, our board made the fearless decision to take a new course.

I remember sitting around the board table, discussing how to make the announcement. We have glass walls at the Case Foundation, and everyone who looked in at us could see our dismay. It was excruciating, because in nonprofit work, people don't want to talk about failure. We discussed backing out quietly, in the hope that perhaps the failure would escape public scrutiny. But in the end, we knew we had to own the fact that the opportunity we were chasing had turned into a challenge we could not meet. We hoped that by acknowledging our shortcomings, we could share lessons that might allow us and others to try new approaches that could work better.

With my heart in my throat, I decided to make the most public pronouncement possible—to name the failure in a written piece, which I titled "The Painful Acknowledgment of Coming Up Short." After I finished writing it, I had a moment of fear as I recognized what a big step it was to announce to the universe, "We failed!"

What I could not have known as I sat there, too terrified to hit the send button, was that once my piece appeared online, I would begin getting emails and phone calls from people across the field thanking me for owning up to the failure in such a public way, and for revealing just how hard it is to get it right when you take on really thorny challenges. Reflecting back on our decision to be so transparent, I realize that, as difficult as it was, that moment represented the beginning of our Be Fearless efforts. And a new suggestion emerged from some of the respondents—the creation of a "safe table" for partners to come together to talk about their own failures, so the learning could be shared. The idea took hold, and some of the early meetings became broader gatherings. They were "fail fests" where we openly recognized that in trying to innovate and solve big problems, we wouldn't always get it right. They represented a commitment to make failure matter by allowing others to learn from our mistakes.

We also changed the way we assessed the outcomes of our work at the Case Foundation, instituting a green-yellow-red assessment scale. Green indicates that things are humming along, yellow that adjustments are needed. Red flags, an effort that may fail. Surprisingly, one annual review when I saw no reds on our various initiatives, I was concerned. I had a frank discussion with the team, pointing out that if we didn't see at least some reds in our portfolio, we weren't being bold enough.

We at the Case Foundation dislike failure as much as anyone, but we know that if we chase extraordinary outcomes, we must take some extraordinary risks. No one gets fired or docked for outcomes that fall short if we are doing our part. Instead, there is a reward for going above and beyond to make Big Bets, take risks, and build unlikely partnerships.

Sometimes pivoting off a failure means helping others win where we ourselves have failed. After we discontinued our support for PlayPumps, we created a new partnership with Water For People, which added PlayPumps as part of a larger portfolio of solutions from which rural African communities could choose. It's a process that philanthropy expert Lucy Bernholz has described as "failing forward."

Since the work of the social sector often directly impacts people, and nonprofits are highly reliant on donor support, there tends to be less tolerance for mistakes, which leads many organizations to become risk-averse, and to hide errors. But when nonprofits aren't transparent about their failures, they deprive others of necessary lessons.

Making failure matter is also important for the private sector. Look at any great business today, and chances are that their road to success included low moments that required fresh thinking and important course corrections. Earlier in this book we introduced the X project, led by Astro Teller. Astro is not just comfortable with the idea of failure—he and his lab are in pursuit of it. Workers at X are expected to fail—it's the way they figure out what works and what doesn't. "The moonshot factory is a messy place," Astro said in an exhilarating TED talk titled "The Unexpected Benefit of Celebrating Failure." "But rather than avoid the mess, pretend it's not there, we've tried to make that our strength. We spend most of our time breaking things and trying to prove that we're wrong. That's it, that's the secret. Run at all the hardest parts of the problem first. Get excited and cheer, 'Hey! How are we going to kill our project today?'"

Astro isn't being facetious. "We work hard at X to make it safe to fail," he says. "Teams kill their ideas as soon as the evidence is on the table because they're rewarded for it. They get applause from their peers. Hugs and high fives from their manager, me in particular. They get promoted for it. We have bonused every single person on teams that ended their projects, from teams as small as two to teams of more than thirty. We believe in dreams at the moonshot factory. But enthusiastic skepticism is not the enemy of boundless optimism. It's optimism's perfect partner." It's not for nothing that Astro has been dubbed "the father of modern failure."

However, Astro is walking in the footsteps of great inventors from long ago. Thomas J. Watson Sr., who built IBM, once said, "If you want to succeed, double your failure rate." Good advice—and he would know. Louis V. Gerstner Jr., who shepherded IBM through the most difficult transition into the computer age and wrote *Who Says Elephants Can't Dance?* about his experiences, tells a story about Watson. In the years just after the Great Depression, Watson increased IBM's inventories, hoping for revived demand for office machinery. He was counting on winning a government bid of a million dollars, a very large sum at the time. But his salesman failed to get the contract. Ashamed, the man showed up in Watson's office and handed him a letter of resignation. "What happened?" Watson asked. The salesman launched into a thorough account of the deal, noting where mistakes had been made and what he might have done differently. When he was finished, Watson handed back the resignation letter and said, "Why would I accept this when I have just invested one million dollars in your education?"

IBM has been a model of fearlessness for over a century. Under Watson's leadership, it provided equal pay for women in 1935 (!) and took a stand against segregation in the American South in 1956, becoming one of the first companies to do so. It was also among the first to include sexual orientation as part of its nondiscrimination policies. Socially responsible and consistently innovative, IBM definitely embodies the spirit of its longtime leader. And today, Ginni Rometty continues this tradition as the first woman to serve as IBM's chair, president, and CEO.

• • •

Meg Whitman, the only woman to have led two major US corporations, has demonstrated her own fearlessness in acknowledging and learning from very public failures. While serving as CEO of eBay in 1998, Meg had a choice—invest in upgrades for eBay's existing website, or invest in a new, emerging Internet market, Japan. She chose the website investment. "That miss of eBay Japan is one of the big failures of my time at eBay," she said in a CNBC interview. At the time, eBay was a young start-up with just $5 million in revenue, and struggling to scale the business. And while the failure cost the company an early lead in an important market, over time under Meg's leadership, the venture grew to more than $8 billion in sales with operations in more than thirty countries.

After eBay, Meg embarked on a run in 2010 for governor of California and failed. Appointed as CEO of Hewlett-Packard after losing her bid for office, she took those failure lessons into her new executive role. "I put everything I had into the campaign," she told CNBC. "But it didn't work out the way I hoped. I learned a lot from it and I think it made me a stronger executive and I think a stronger person."

The question each of us must ask ourselves is whether in the face of failure we would try again. Maybe you've never failed and you think this advice isn't relevant to you. But you *will* someday. And I *want* you to fail. Fail fast, fail forward, make it matter, and then go do something really, really great.

Do I like failure? I detest failure. The point isn't to glorify failure or to use it as an excuse, but rather to acknowledge that achievements usually follow it. So if it happens, let it teach you, and then allow the experience of overcoming it to energize you and lead to success. Failure only becomes a positive when you do something with it.

TWELVE

FAIL IN THE FOOTSTEPS OF GIANTS

Albert Einstein is credited with saying, "Failure is success in progress." But many people have a hard time accepting that their failures can mean anything other than embarrassment and loss. I understand that. We're so schooled in the language of success that mistakes can seem like life-ruining events. When something goes wrong, the first thing everyone wants to know is who's to blame. I doubt that the Hawaii Emergency Management Agency employee who erroneously pushed a nuclear alert button in January 2018 will put that on his résumé. But his mistake led to improvements in the system that could save lives.

Many of the people we most admire built their successes on top of failures, because those failures sparked great turnarounds. When a young Oprah Winfrey co-anchored the local news at WJZ-TV in Baltimore, viewers didn't know what to make of her. She became used to hearing "What's an Oprah?" Her co-anchor resented being paired with her, and the station dropped her from the desk after only seven and a half months. It was a very public failure and hard to recover from. She still remembers feeling humiliated and devastated. But then the station stuck her on a floundering talk show called *People Are Talking*, and Oprah learned that she had a gift she hadn't known about. In the talk format, her personality and warmth shone through. Today Oprah is one of the most powerful business executives in the world, and she says she got that way by being true to herself. In a commencement address at Harvard University in 2013, she told the students, "Failure is just life trying to move us in another direction. Now, when you're down there in the hole, it looks like failure. . . . And when you're down in the hole, when that moment comes, it's really okay to feel bad for a little while. Give yourself time to mourn what you think you may have lost, but then, here's the key, learn from every mistake, because every experience, encounter, and particularly your mistakes are there to teach you and force you into being more who you are. And then figure out what is the next right move. And the key to life is to develop an internal moral, emotional GPS that can tell you which way to go."

> *"Do the one thing you think you cannot do. Fail at it. Try again. The only people who never tumble are those who never mount the high wire."*
>
> —OPRAH WINFREY

Rejection is painful, but it can spark creativity. Steven Spielberg was often lonely as a child. Growing up an Orthodox Jew, he has said he often felt alienated from his classmates, and was regularly bullied. He dreamed of becoming a filmmaker, and made small home movies. But he struggled in school—he suffered from dyslexia—and graduated from high school with a C average. His application to the University of Southern California film school was rejected, and he settled for California State University in Long Beach, where he got an internship at Universal Studios. There his talent blossomed, and he was given a directing contract. He dropped out of school and began his film career.

Today Steven is heralded for hits like *E. T.*, *Jaws*, *Raiders of the Lost Ark*, *Schindler's List*, and *Saving Private Ryan*. (*E.T.*, which at its heart is about lost and lonely children, was inspired by his parents' divorce.) But he's had his share of flops as well; we just don't hear about them. Critics unanimously panned his 1979 World War II comedy *1941*, for example. But Steven says that he's proud of every movie he's ever made. He's able to embrace calamity as grist for creativity. In his words, "Once a month the sky falls on my head, I come to, and I see another movie I want to make."

• • •

A teacher once pronounced Thomas Edison "too stupid to learn," and his early professional life was hardly auspicious, with a number of significant failures. He reportedly was fired from several early jobs. So how did he have the strength to keep going? He credited his mother with giving him an outsized sense of confidence. But even so, after thousands of false starts on the lightbulb, Edison was such a famous flop that, as the story is frequently told, a newspaper reporter once asked him if he was ready to give up. He replied, "I haven't failed. I've just found ten thousand ways that won't work. Success is almost in my grasp." He didn't give up, and the rest is history.

Yet lest you get the idea that failure reliably precedes success, consider Steve Jobs, the revolutionary founder of Apple. Steve experienced his biggest failure *after* he'd already achieved success. Think about it. He started Apple in his garage with his buddy Steve Wozniak, launching the first Apple computer in 1976. In 1980 the company went public. There were some ups and downs along the way—the 1983 Apple Lisa was a notable flop. But the innovative Macintosh was introduced the next year.

Even as Apple became corporate, Steve kept his nontraditional spirit. And so, in 1985, a new CEO orchestrated a very public ousting of Steve from the company he'd founded. Twenty years later, at a commencement speech at Stanford, Steve spoke about the terrible pain of that experience. But he went on to say, "I didn't see it then, but it turned out that getting fired from Apple was the best thing that could have ever happened to me. The heaviness of being successful was replaced by the lightness of being a beginner again, less sure about everything. It freed me to enter one of the most creative periods of my life."

Steve would return to Apple as CEO in 1997, and he continued to be a rebel until the day he died in 2011 at the age of fifty-six. One of Apple's most famous advertising campaigns, "Think Different," was an ode to those who didn't fit, who dared to be different and even outrageous. "While some see them as the crazy ones, we see genius. Because the people who are crazy enough to think they can change the world are the ones who do."

One of Steve's most profitable investments during his years away from Apple was in a company called Pixar, which had its own history of building success from failure. Steve helped transform it into a company Disney was eager to buy. (Incidentally, Walt Disney was another failure-to-success story, getting fired from an early job with a Missouri newspaper for "not being creative enough," and then going on to start Laugh-o-Gram Studio, which went bankrupt.) Ed Catmull, Pixar's cofounder, once said in an interview, "We need to think about failure differently. I'm not the first to say that failure, when approached properly, can be an opportunity for growth. But the way most people interpret this assertion is that mistakes are a necessary evil. Mistakes aren't a necessary evil. They aren't evil at all. They are an inevitable consequence of doing something new, and, as such, should be seen as valuable; without them, we'd have no originality. And yet, even as I say that embracing failure is an important part of learning, I also realize that acknowledging this truth is not enough. That's because failure is painful, and our feelings about this pain tend to screw up our understanding of its worth. To disentangle the good and the bad parts of failure, we have to recognize both the reality of the pain and the benefit of the resulting growth."

Sports provide daily lessons in overcoming failure, because competing in a sport means losing at least some of the time. When our kids compete in sports, we have plenty of opportunities to help them deal with failure. The first lesson: you will have another day. This is one of the few arenas where we are told, especially when we are first learning, that it is okay to fall, crash, trip, or drop the ball so we can improve. That is one of the elements that make sports so remarkable in our society. In sports, failure and learning from that failure are integral to success.

That lesson doesn't end on the playground. Many of the greatest athletes in the world continue to lose frequently—as anyone who has ever watched a Super Bowl, a World Series game, or an NBA championship knows. "I've missed more than nine thousand shots in my career," Michael Jordan has said. "I've lost almost three hundred games. Twenty-six times I've been trusted to take the game-winning shot and missed. I've failed over and over and over again in my life. And that is why I succeed." Or, as tennis great Serena Williams put it, "I really think a champion is defined not by their wins, but by how they can recover when they fall."

Athletes also face another, more grievous kind of failure: career-ending injuries. Kelly Clark was the most decorated Olympic snowboarder when she crashed at the 2015 X Games in Norway, tearing her hamstring from the bone and ripping the cartilage that kept her femur in her hip joint. She spent the next month in bed with her feet bound together and, after surgery, had to relearn how to walk. Others in her position might have taken their medals and retired gracefully, but Kelly refused to let the injury define her career by ending it. She made the bold decision to recover, train, and compete again—not just to win, but to give others hope.

Kelly astounded the sports world by qualifying for the 2018 Olympics in PyeongChang, becoming the first snowboarder to compete in five Olympic games. And she did it at the age of thirty-four, competing against challengers half her age. Although she didn't win a medal, she finished just below third place. Watching the PyeongChang games, I noticed how much other athletes, including Chloe Kim, who won the gold medal, look up to Clark.

• • •

Richard Branson's failures are legendary. When launching his first, most high-profile venture, Virgin Atlantic Airways, he had only one plane, which was ambushed by a flock of birds on its test run. Over time, he's started many businesses, some of them spectacular bombs—such as Virgin Cola, designed to take on Coke, and Virgin Cars, an online car-selling business. But Branson kept coming back. He epitomizes the entrepreneurial spirit of fail, regroup, and start something else. Today Branson's Virgin Group is an umbrella for some four hundred companies. "If you fall flat on your face, at least you're moving forward," he has said.

When we think about the phrase "following in the footsteps of others," rarely do we associate those footsteps with failure. But this chapter was written specifically to demonstrate that extraordinary leaders and high achievers have failed on their own paths to success, sometimes time and time again. So the next time you fail, remember that you are failing in the footsteps of giants.

THIRTEEN

BEAT THE ODDS

Throughout my life, there have been moments when I have been keenly aware of being different from those around me, whether because of my background or gender or education—the types of differences that could contribute to a sense of inferiority, or perhaps cause me to develop what's called the impostor syndrome, a sense that I'm not worthy of my standing and am just faking it.

In too many settings through the years, I was the only student on financial aid. Later, I was the only one without a college degree, or the only woman at the board table. You get the idea. For those who are made to feel "different" in society, the fear of failure can be particularly paralyzing, because we can fear that we'll let our entire similar *class* down.

Oddly, however, this sense of disenfranchisement can be a force multiplier. Those with "something to prove"—those whom others would count out because they don't fit the mold—often excel to extraordinary heights. Like a woman named Oprah, like a young Thomas Edison who didn't seem teachable, like Steven Spielberg, rejected from film school.

At her lowest, J. K. Rowling, the phenomenal best-selling author of the Harry Potter series, was a single mother on welfare, struggling with depression. She was, she later said, the biggest failure she knew. This dark chapter of her life inspired the mysterious world of good and evil that is the basis of her novels. She began to write in longhand at night, sitting in coffee shops, and when she finally dared to submit her work to publishers, she received rejection after rejection.

In 2016, Rowling posted some of these early rejection letters on Twitter as a way of inspiring hopeful writers to not give up. When respondents asked how she had the motivation to keep trying, she replied, "I had nothing to lose, and sometimes that makes you brave enough to try." Many budding authors posted grateful responses on Twitter, writing that the story of her early rejections gave them the courage to go on.

• • •

In 1985, Sudan was caught up in a brutal civil war. Millions died and millions more were displaced. When eleven-year-old Salva Dut's village in South Sudan was attacked, he ran for his life with the other boys, some as young as five, walking hundreds of miles to a refugee camp in Ethiopia. They and others like them became known as the Lost Boys of Sudan, but "We weren't really lost," Salva said in a TED talk about his experience. "We were the walking boys." They encountered lions on land and crocodiles in the water, but their greatest fear was being found by soldiers who would kill them to prevent them from growing up to become resistance fighters.

When the boys finally reached the camp, they found that the conditions were nearly unlivable—one scoop of food a day, little

water, and no sanitation. Worst of all, there were no adult caretak-
ers; the Lost Boys had to fend for themselves. They decided they
couldn't stay, so at age fifteen, Salva was elected to lead 1,500 boys
to the Kakuma refugee camp in Kenya, a journey of hundreds of
miles across rough terrain. There, conditions improved.

At age twenty-two, Salva came to America as a political refugee
and settled with a family in Rochester, New York. He had to learn
how to do everything from turning on a light switch to shopping
at a grocery store. And then one day, a few years after arriving in
the United States, Salva learned some stunning news: his father,
whom he had been certain had died in the war, was alive. He traveled to South Sudan to reunite with a parent he hadn't seen since
he was eleven, only to find his father critically ill from drinking
contaminated water. When Salva described the water in his TED
talk, he pulled a plastic bottle out of his pocket and held it up so
the audience could see the muddy brew.

Salva returned to the United States and, knowing nothing about
philanthropy, started a nonprofit called Water for South Sudan to
commence the battle to provide safe drinking water for the community he had fled. It took him four years to raise $50,000 to drill
a well in his father's village. Since that first well in 2005, Water
for South Sudan has drilled 304 wells in remote villages, serving
hundreds of thousands of people. Salva's story is memorable on
many levels, but hope and perseverance are messages he continu-
ally expresses. The theme of his life is walking—a metaphor for
persistence. Today, when he encounters hardship, he says, "I just
keep walking, putting one foot in front of another. I learned if you
keep persisting, you will accomplish many good things in your life,
in any terrible circumstances."

Stories like Salva's inspire us, but what of others in our midst who feel lost? We call our military veterans heroes, yet while we applaud their courage at war, we often have too little to offer them when they return home, as Barbara Van Dahlen reminds us. Many soldiers suffer traumatic injuries on the battlefield, and at least 20 percent of Iraq and Afghanistan veterans suffer from PTSD. Too many brave soldiers have trouble reintegrating, lacking the community and the sense of purpose that once defined their daily lives. Their failure to thrive can manifest in many ways, most painfully in the high rates of veteran suicide and homelessness.

Enter Team Rubicon. When a 7.0 magnitude earthquake struck Port-au-Prince, Haiti, in January 2010, nearly 1 million Haitians were left homeless and thousands died. Jake Wood and William McNulty, two former US Marines, jumped in to help. Along with six other veterans and friends, they gathered funds and medical supplies, flew to the Dominican Republic, loaded a truck with supplies, and drove to Haiti. In the process of providing disaster relief, Team Rubicon found it could also provide veterans with a way to regain their sense of self-worth by giving them a fresh purpose and a new community.

At first, the members of Team Rubicon saw themselves as a disaster relief organization that was using veteran services. Then Clay Hunt, an original member of Team Rubicon, took his own life. After Hunt's death, they began to see themselves as a veteran services organization that was using disaster relief. As Jake Wood said in a moving talk, in which he spoke of his friend and about pride and loss in the lives of military veterans: "You have an eighteen-year-old boy who graduates high school in Kansas City. He joins the Army. The Army gives him a rifle. They send him to Iraq. They pin a medal on his chest. He goes home to a ticker-tape parade. He takes the uniform off. He's no longer Sergeant Jones in his community. He's now Dave from Kansas City. He doesn't have that same self-worth. But you send him to Joplin [Missouri] after a tornado, and somebody once again is walking up to him and shaking [his] hand and thanking [him] for [his] service, now [he has] self-worth again."

• • •

It is not too often that I meet other leaders in the privileged world of philanthropy who share a background like mine—having previously been a *recipient* of philanthropy before taking the helm of a foundation. So when I first met Darren Walker and heard the remarkable story of how he beat the odds to become president of the Ford Foundation, one of the largest foundations in the United States, I was deeply touched. Despite the Ford Foundation's tradition, prestige, and sheer size (with assets over $12 billion), Darren speaks openly about his challenged upbringing: "I embrace my past," he told Jonathan Capehart in a moving interview published in the *Washington Post*. "I didn't have to study the context of a low-income, rural community to know about poverty. I lived that experience."

Darren, now a dear friend, knows he occupies a rare place, having overcome significant odds. He is a gay black man from the South, yet at no time did he allow bias or other daunting hurdles to keep him from achieving his dreams. Darren's unique life story is an inspiration to many and has led to numerous profiles that tell his story, including *Time* magazine naming him one of the 100 Most Influential People in the World. He encourages others who achieve status or privilege to speak out, to empower others, and to make a difference. "I'm very, very optimistic about America's future," he likes to say, and with stories like Darren's to inspire us, we are reminded that anyone can beat the odds.

Perhaps you feel the burden of what others will say if you stumble, especially if you're like me and think your failure could play into the bias that exists around who is and who isn't expected to do something great. I want to encourage you to focus on the people highlighted in this chapter, who not only felt disenfranchised or different but actually were. And yet each one of them overcame their fear of being called out for their failures. In so doing, they've not only achieved great things—they've helped to reduce bias when we think about the potential of those who are "different." Let their stories inspire you to overcome the insecurity that could otherwise hold you back.

FOURTEEN

TAKE THE LONG VIEW

I wish I'd known when I didn't get into the college of my choice that staying local would lead to a job in Washington with the Reagan administration. I wish I had known when that job was suspended for lack of funding and I took a temporary job at a tech start-up to pay rent, that this new job would lead me to a career I couldn't have imagined. When I look back, I can still recall the bitter disappointment I felt on both occasions—along with the fear that I would never find a place for myself. If only I'd had a crystal ball.

Every life has many chapters. The wise person can see the new opportunities that sprout out of disappointments. The wise organization can too. I once read about a founder who kept plans for the next big idea for his company on a piece of paper in his desk drawer—waiting for the moment when he thought the conditions were right. On some level, this could be wise. But there's also never the perfect time to try something audacious. If you wait too long, the moment might just pass you by. Yes, timing is everything, but as the proverb states, "The best time to plant a tree was twenty years ago; the next best time is now."

Timing and outside factors can play a big role in the success of an idea—and also in its failure. It is important to be clear headed about the realities of taking the risk to start something new, as many people, companies, and entities try big things and fail. We all must acknowledge that failure does happen and some of that is inevitable. For every Facebook, there is a Friendster; for every Spotify, there is a Napster; for every entity that successfully funds breakthroughs in brain cancer, there are labs filled with dedicated doctors and technicians who will not make a significant impact on the health of the next generation.

Sometimes failures happen not because an idea is bad, but because the execution is wrong. Talk to any successful founder of a business or movement and they'll often remember early days when they had too little time, few resources, and talent that was less than world-class. The key is identifying the potential for failure early on so that you can course-correct before it's too late. It's important to have an honest discussion about what's working and what's not, and to tap others to help you identify what's wrong and make necessary adjustments along the way.

The Gates Foundation announced in 2006 that it was committing $13 billion to eradicating polio by 2010. It was an audacious plan, but they believed they could do it, and those who joined their effort believed the same. By 2010, however, polio was spreading in some of the very countries targeted for eradication.

I felt their pain because I've been there myself—albeit at a different level. Imagine investing such a significant sum out of the goodness of your heart, committing your time and the talents of people you admire. And then imagine learning that your efforts didn't work. It was a blow for Bill Gates, but rather than wallowing in the defeat, he took the long view. "What do we do next?" he asked. It was exactly the right question. The Gates Foundation team kept going, kept working, kept investing. As of this writing, the Gates Foundation says there are only twelve cases of poliovirus remaining in two countries, and the goal shared by Bill and Melinda Gates is in sight. The key is that they never doubted they were on the right track. They never considered bailing. They took the long view and figured out what it would take to get the job done, despite the setbacks along the way.

In sports, we've often seen the need to take the long view as failures or shortcomings stack up. Take, for instance, the story of Ted Leonsis, owner of the Washington Capitals hockey team. Ted had been a good friend and colleague at AOL, having joined the company after it acquired a technology firm he'd founded. Everyone knew Ted as a bright, capable leader with great vision, and a portfolio of outstanding achievements. When Ted bought the Washington Capitals in 1999, he had a singular focus: win the Stanley Cup. Yet despite acquiring a deep bench of elite players, winning the NHL's Presidents' Trophy for racking up the most points during the regular season three times since 2010, and making multiple appearances in the NHL playoffs, the team failed to bring the Stanley Cup to Washington, DC, for almost twenty years. In much the same way that Ted sees the entrepreneurship that has been at the center of his career, he kept pushing for success, making the adjustments necessary to keep the campaign on track and never losing confidence in the overall mission. Proof of the fans' support throughout this period can be seen at the box office, where—even without making the Stanley Cup finals—the Capitals sold out more than four hundred straight games.

Then, finally, in 2018, Ted and his team pulled it off. They won the Stanley Cup, marking the first time in history the Cup came to Washington, DC. In the midst of the celebration, when asked about the long road to victory, Ted noted, "It is much, much sweeter to go through all the pain and suffering to get to the top of the mountain. That's the way life is. That's the way great businesses get built. It is never easy."

•　•　•

I often look to the past to appreciate the wisdom of taking the long view. Before you label someone a failure, think about Milton S. Hershey. Born in 1857 in rural Pennsylvania to a father who abandoned the family and a long-suffering mother who needed her son's support, Hershey had little chance for formal education. At fourteen, he went to work for a confectioner in Lancaster to learn the art of candy making. After four years of apprenticeship, Hershey decided to strike out on his own, aided by a $150 loan from his aunt. He moved to Philadelphia and began his life as a candy-making entrepreneur. Despite his passion and perseverance, his business failed within five years. Frustrated but undaunted, Hershey joined his father in Denver and set out to learn another confectioner's craft: making caramel. He thought this new candy would take the nation by storm, and he traveled across America, finally settling in New York City, where at twenty-six he opened his own candy store; it closed within three years.

When Hershey returned home to Pennsylvania, his family thought he was a drifter. They didn't even want him to attend a family reunion. He was now approaching forty with nothing to show for his efforts. Was it time to give up his entrepreneurial dreams?

He didn't. Instead, he launched the Lancaster Caramel Company. His mother and aunt helped him experiment with "melt in your mouth" recipes, and at last his company was successful. When he sold the Lancaster Caramel Company in 1900 for a million dollars, he had a grander ambition: chocolate.

Chocolate candy was hardly new, but the technology for mass production was, and Hershey invested in the latest equipment to open the Hershey Chocolate Company in his hometown of Derry Park. (The town was later renamed Hershey.) Perhaps influenced by the hardships he had known, he devised a plan to build Hershey into a model town where his workers could enjoy life—a place where they could live, work, and play in relative comfort. Finally, he had achieved his dream.

But Hershey had more to offer the world. Prior to building the Hershey Chocolate Company, he met the woman to whom he would devote the rest of his life—his wife, Catherine. When the Hersheys discovered they couldn't have children, the couple decided to focus their philanthropic endeavors on children in need. They opened the Hershey Industrial School for orphaned boys, a vocational school that Hershey hoped would teach students skills that would enable them to land well-paying jobs. After Catherine died in 1915, Hershey transferred the majority of his assets to the school. Today more than two thousand underserved students each year call the Milton Hershey School (which now admits girls) home. It wasn't until 1989 that the school stopped requiring students to milk cows twice a day, a directive provided by Hershey at the school's founding. Due to his forethought, the school enjoys an endowment of $12.5 billion, more than some Ivy League universities.

• • •

There's a term for people who achieve success later in life: late bloomers. "On the road to great achievement, the late bloomer will resemble a failure," Malcolm Gladwell wrote in the *New Yorker*, an insight that would surely apply to Hershey. We're biased to think that youth have an advantage at creativity and dreaming big. Yet late bloomers can also be successful if they have the right attitude and a healthy perspective about the future.

While we recognize the role that urgency can play in making a Big Bet, sometimes the long view is what counts. It's important to put failure in perspective. A strikeout in the first inning needs to be considered in the context of the whole game ahead. (It's been said Babe Ruth was the home run king, but he was also the strikeout king.) Too many companies stumble because they worry about this quarter's earnings, not their longer-term vision.

Warren Buffett is an extraordinarily successful leader and a business guru to many. In recent years I have had the pleasure of spending time with Warren at the annual Giving Pledge gathering, and in other business or conference settings. The Giving Pledge was formed in 2010 by Bill and Melinda Gates, together with Warren, and represents a network of individuals and families who have committed to give away the bulk of their wealth. Steve and I had had the benefit of knowing Bill and Melinda during our early technology years, but we hadn't come to know Warren very well prior to joining this group. I always look forward with great anticipation to spending time with Warren, often referred to as the Oracle of Omaha. Warren uses these gatherings to share the wisdom he has acquired throughout his eighty-eight years and to bring a sense of humor and lightness to meetings with a very serious interest in addressing daunting challenges around the world.

Warren is the third-wealthiest person in the world. However, he readily admits that he's made his share of costly mistakes. He is well known for the strength of Berkshire Hathaway, yet he told CNBC in 2010 that the "dumbest stock I ever bought was Berkshire Hathaway." He went on to explain that he only purchased significant holdings in the company, at that time a shrinking textile business, due to a slight by its CEO, and that the performance of the textile company was a drag on all the other investments that he later made under the Berkshire Hathaway name. In that interview, he estimated that the cost of purchasing Berkshire Hathaway for the wrong reasons had been considerable! But the Oracle of Omaha has recovered from his failures by a strategy of longview investing—not buying and selling with shifts in the winds, but rather looking for businesses that will build long-term value. In fact, his entire life is defined by the long view. Did you know that Buffett earned most of his fortune after his fiftieth birthday? And between the ages of eighty-three and eighty-seven, he saw his wealth grow by as much as he earned in his first sixty-six years of life. In many ways Buffet is exceptional—yet as individuals, we can choose to adopt the same approach.

The stories in this chapter were specifically chosen to demonstrate the importance of perseverance as you encounter failure along the way. With each twist and turn and failure, we're stronger if we keep our eye on the prize, even if it takes a while to arrive.

FIFTEEN

NOW GO, LEARN FROM FAILURE

Making a Big Bet requires the risk of failure. As the stories we've shared illustrating this principle have shown, every great innovator has failed, but only the truly great among them find ways to apply the lessons of their failures to propel them forward. Ask yourself if failure, or the fear of failure, is getting in your way.

It's human nature to want to hide your failures because they feel embarrassing. You said you'd achieve something, and you fell short. But what if instead of burrowing into a hole of shame, you stood up, announced your failure, and used the opportunity to say what you've learned and to reaffirm your commitment to your goal? I can't stress enough how freeing this is—a lesson I've learned from stumbles along the way.

Likewise, rejection is painful, but in hindsight it can be a badge of honor. This is a lesson we can take from innovators and leaders who recognize, as Einstein did, that their failures bring them that much closer to future success. J. K. Rowling kept trying despite rejection. Astro Teller built failure into the success mix. And Warren Buffett reminds us to keep at it for the long term. Whenever you experience a setback, let the wisdom from these great achievers help you get back up again.

Jeff Bezos wrote to Amazon shareholders in 2014, "Failure comes part and parcel with invention. It's not optional. We understand that and believe in failing early and iterating until we get it right." He was reiterating what Thomas Edison said so long ago.

Take a moment now to consider your own life. Perhaps you have a story of failure—a time when it seemed you would never recover from a deep disappointment. Can you now appreciate the gift of that experience? What did you learn from that dark time? What future opportunity did it unveil?

> *"For every failure, there's an alternative course of action. You just have to find it. When you come to a roadblock, take a detour."*
> —MARY KAY ASH

I believe that perfection—that is, *never failing*—is a myth. There's tremendous pressure in our culture to be perfect, and this impacts young people most of all. To get into the best schools these days, you need not only perfect grades but also a perfect résumé of nonacademic achievements. Then, to get a good job, you need a perfect grade point average, plus internships and more extracurricular activities. No wonder the American Psychological Association has reported that the stress of trying to be perfect is contributing to a rise in depression among teenagers.

The story of the Gates Foundation's efforts in polio eradication teaches us a very important lesson. When you fall short, ask,

"What do we do next?" The road to success is a long journey, with peaks and valleys and boulders in your path. As you set out for your destination, remember and embrace the wise words of Ernest Shackleton, the Antarctic explorer, mentioned earlier: "Difficulties are just things to overcome, after all."

PART FOUR

REACH BEYOND
YOUR BUBBLE

Eliminate blind spots

Build unlikely partnerships

Be better together

Leverage partnerships for growth

Now go, get outside your bubble . . . every day

SIXTEEN

ELIMINATE BLIND SPOTS

"Where are you?" The voice of a business associate came through the Bluetooth connection in my vehicle. "Steve and I are driving through Pennsylvania on an RV road trip," I answered. This was an important business call, and my husband and I had agreed I should take it, even though it had caught us as we were heading off for vacation. My associate's disbelief was obvious. "I'm shocked," he said. "Why would the two of you do something like that?"

Since becoming empty nesters, Steve and I have set off each August with a camper van in tow in pursuit of life's simplest pleasures, such as the beauty of a rolling countryside and the down-to-earth joy of a dinner made by campfire. We also keep a pack of quarters handy to pay for three minutes of hot showers we sometimes use along the way.

As we roll from site to site, we explore small towns, local haunts, monuments, and parks, discovering the tapestry of America. For us, these road trips are an expedition. Despite my working-class Midwest roots, Steve and I now live a privileged life in the Washington, DC, area, so these trips help us build connections with people and places that can be quite different from what has become familiar to us. We encounter people who are often judged or dismissed by those on the coasts. But we've found that no matter where we go, a new perspective is acquired and an abiding respect develops. Sometimes we simply come to appreciate the challenges and opportunities of places that are so often overlooked or misunderstood.

On a recent trip, we were enjoying a sunny and surprisingly crisp August day in the coal country of eastern Pennsylvania when reviews of local eateries led us to a bar/restaurant in a once-thriving mining town. We drove down Main Street, which showed signs of blight and abandonment. It's not very often that we find enough empty parking spaces to fit our rig on a town's main street, but in this case, we had our pick. Having parked neatly along the curb, I hopped out to fill the meter.

We proceeded down the block to the M & M Redzone, a sports bar that boasted five stars on Yelp and was ranked #1 on TripAdvisor. As we sat down, the owner, Bobby Moucheron, came over to offer advice on the menu. He recommended the Philly cheesesteak and the special chicken wings, and that's what we ordered. While we waited for our food, we asked about the town and about his own story. Like all American stories, Bobby's was full of twists and turns. He'd been born and raised in town but left after college to work for a telephone company in a job that no longer exists—he was a telephone operator. There, he was given the chance to be trained on the then-new technology of PBX systems, a good career path that took him through to his recent retirement. Back in Mahanoy City, an opportunity came to buy the M & M, and he took it. His great-great-grandfather had once owned the place.

Mahanoy City speaks to the challenges faced by communities

across the nation. Once thriving—reportedly the home to more bars per capita than any other place in America—it is today a town trying desperately to fight its way back. The economic decline and related issues—drugs, unemployment, low wages—are hard to reckon with for someone like Bobby, who came home in hopes of a new future for his hometown. While the US Census puts the median household income in the US at $59,000, it records Mahanoy County at $27,000. And yet the week we passed through town, Bobby's Facebook page was filled with photos of donations from his friends and neighbors to the victims of Hurricane Harvey in Texas. We came looking for America and we found it: a struggling community giving what it has to benefit others who are even worse off.

During our 1,800-mile journey, meandering through the small towns of Pennsylvania, New York, and Virginia, we saw the face of America in many intimate encounters. There were those who were blunt about the lack of hope they saw. For example, at one stop we were greeted by a woman who exclaimed, "I don't know what you're doing here, but if you had any sense you'd get right back in your truck and go back to where you came from. Nothing good comes from this town." But for every negative comment we heard, there were two or three positive ones that offered unique perspectives and made us smile. Like the Mennonite family of nine home-schooled kids that operates an organic store along the highway, or the mother of two preschoolers who, when learning of our RV camping trip and nights spent at beautiful state parks, was filled with admiration. "Why," she asked, "would anyone pay a fortune to stay in hotel rooms when the most beautiful places are in our state and national parks, and only cost twenty to thirty dollars a night?" She had a point.

One of our last stops was at the breakfast spot ranked number one on all the crowdsourced sites. As we rolled off the highway and into a small town on the Susquehanna River, we realized that the highly rated dining spot was inside a pharmacy, and there was a line out the door. When we finally got inside, we found a bustling classic counter. We felt as though we'd checked in to a different era. As folks came and went, they greeted each other by name, and asked about family or commented on local happenings. This, we thought, was the spirit of community so many people yearn for in our modern era of technology and mobility.

Our annual RV trip along the back roads of America is a way for us to expand our understanding beyond our bubble, to reduce our blind spots or biases about people who live differently than we do. Study after study confirms that we all have biases of one kind or another. So if you seek to be a changemaker, you have to broaden your understanding of the world. There's no other way.

In 2017, my friend and longtime colleague Ross Baird wrote a book called *The Innovation Blind Spot*. The book portrays the current state of entrepreneurship, investment, and innovation in the United States, with a focus on the blind spots that inhibit growth and opportunity. Ross reminds us that although entrepreneurship is what sets us apart as a nation, it turns out that entrepreneurial activity is actually at a forty-year low in the US. More businesses die each day than start.

Sure, there are sectors that are thriving in our "innovation nation"—particularly big companies and those elites who have historically had access to capital and networks. But others across the country are being left behind in the innovation economy, particularly women, people of color, those in the middle of the country, and those from lower-income backgrounds. Ross, who has joined every one of my husband, Steve's, Rise of the Rest road trips, understands the hurdles this poses for innovators who come from diverse backgrounds or heartland communities. His book seems in many respects like a companion to Adam Grant's *Originals* or my husband's 2016 book, *The Third Wave*. As all of these books make clear, great innovations come from unexpected people and places, and together serve as a clarion call to the rest of us to pay attention to what's happening beyond our own backyards.

Another regular on Steve's Rise of the Rest tours is J. D. Vance, the best-selling author of *Hillbilly Elegy*, which was one of the most-read books of 2016 and continues to be a best-seller. Vance, who grew up poor in Middletown, Ohio, has a special gift for articulating truths about the values of people in the heartland, helping us all understand their challenges and the contributions they make in our society. He is a welcome partner on Steve's entrepreneurial mission.

Eliminating blind spots in our mind-sets and our organizations can feel daunting, but it can also represent a powerful opportunity to broaden our perspective and may lead to new and novel solutions. Consider how we refer to the vast middle of the nation as "flyover country," as if its merits don't warrant serious attention. This closed-mindedness limits our potential as a nation. It also runs counter to our history, as the story of America is one of people coming from all places and backgrounds to take forward the next big idea.

• • •

The former steel town of Pittsburgh is thought of by many as the victim of a dying industry. But Pittsburgh, I found on a recent visit, is a unique combination of start-up accelerators, universities, tech companies, and investors intent on creating the city's resurgence. This is the reason Ford pledged to invest $1 billion over five years in a Pittsburgh-based company specializing in artificial intelligence and autonomous car engineering. It is the reason Uber has invested in Pittsburgh as a hub for its autonomous vehicle technology. Pittsburgh innovators range from Courtney Williamson, the founder of AbiliLife, a biomedical company that engineers devices for Parkinson's patients; to Vaish Krishnamurthy of CleanRobotics, whose Trashbot uses artificial intelligence to sort recyclables from waste; to Matthew Stanton and Hahna Alexander, cofounders of Sole-Power, a technology that uses a foot-powered, energy-generating insole to charge portable devices—something of particular interest to the US Army.

Detroit is also experiencing an epic rebirth, led by visionaries like Quicken Loans founder Dan Gilbert, who moved his company and all of its employees to the city after the 2008 economic crisis. He has invested heavily in Detroit real estate, helped dozens of start-ups, and now employs an estimated 17,000 people. Detroit's renaissance is also thanks to unlikely collaborations between the public and private sectors—particularly leading philanthropies, including the Kresge, Ford, and Kellogg Foundations, whose commitment to bringing all sectors of society to the table has been key to the broad impact the city's economic and social revitalization has had. Because of these joint efforts, Detroit is fighting its way back, and the optimism coming from this city sets a great model for others. New skills and a new way of thinking about work are being created in the shadow of the once-great automobile industry.

• • •

Often, the very nature of being in a bubble means you don't know you're in it. It takes intention and effort to shake loose from complacency, to get outside and look around. Comedian Tina Fey, commenting on her experience in the *Saturday Night Live* writing room, noted that when the writers were all or mostly male, it meant fewer skits for and about women. It wasn't purposeful discrimination, just what happens when you exclude other voices. When more women had seats at the writers' table, more stories written by women and about female experiences made it on the air.

Reach Beyond Your Bubble calls on you to seek out those with different perspectives and backgrounds as you take forward your Big Bet. The ability to work with and understand people who are not like you is part of the secret sauce of success.

SEVENTEEN

BUILD UNLIKELY PARTNERSHIPS

There is an old saying that two heads are better than one, and, of course, it's true that more brainpower alone can be a good thing. But the phrase also hits on something not well understood by most people when they think about breakthroughs. As I've said before, too often creativity is seen as the stuff of a lone genius, when in reality great organizations, products, and movements have been advanced by the collaborations between people who are quite different from one another, and who complement one another's skills. These kinds of collaborations give projects a powerful competitive advantage.

And research supports this. In 2015, McKinsey's *Diversity Matters* report looked at a wide range of financial metrics and the composition of the top management and boards of 366 public companies across a range of industries in Canada, Latin America, the UK, and the US, and found that companies with more gender or racial and ethnic diversity were more likely to perform better financially. This was true across the board: companies with the most significant racial and ethnic diversity were 35 percent more likely to have financial returns above the median return for their country, and those with the strongest gender diversity performed 15 percent better than their counterparts. In the United States, they found a direct correlation between diversity and performance, with every 10 percent increase in racial and ethnic diversity yielding a 0.8 percent rise in earnings. These diverse companies are examples of the benefit of forming unlikely partnerships.

When I guest-lecture in business schools, I love to tell a story about how the National Geographic Society reached beyond its bubble in a totally surprising way. Actually, National Geographic's core mission has always been to reach out, tapping awesome explorers, photographers, scientists, and storytellers from around the world to go to the front lines of the unknown and tell the world what they have found. In my travels with National Geographic Explorers, I have climbed mountain peaks in the Himalayas in search of the world's highest temple, dived to the depths of the ocean floor, and gone into the field to observe threatened species across continents. But the exhilarating work of National Geographic Explorers, and our ability to find and fund important work taking place across the planet, is only made possible by a unique partnership.

> *"If you want to go fast, go alone.*
> *If you want to go far, go together."*
> —AFRICAN PROVERB

Shortly after the National Geographic Society was founded one winter night in Washington, DC, in 1888, the Society elected to produce a scientific journal to cover the exploits of scientists and explorers across the world, and to use the proceeds from the magazine's sales to provide funding for more explorers and scientists. I like to say that *National Geographic* may have been the first social enterprise!

Fast-forward through time. This same enterprise model is alive and prospering. In 2015, a new, unlikely partnership was formed with 21st Century Fox to house the National Geographic cable channels, magazine, and digital offerings. It's not intuitive to think about a nonprofit partnering with a major media and entertainment company; both Fox and National Geographic had to reach outside their comfort zones—Fox to work with a nonprofit, and National Geographic to work with a company whose content ranged from sports to movies. But this new partnership has allowed National Geographic content to reach nearly a billion people across the globe each month. Today the organization's endowment is $1.3 billion, and more than $100 million flows out of the joint venture annually, enabling the National Geographic Society to continue its tradition of funding important science, exploration, education, and storytelling around the globe—strengthening and securing the brand and business model along the way.

Co-branding is not a new idea, but reaching beyond your bubble requires more than collaboration between two obviously compatible organizations. There's no question that such collaborations can be daring. They require each side to give up some measure of control, to compromise while maintaining their values. But when those from different domains do form new entities, the result can be magical, accomplishing far more than either could do on their own.

> *"No matter how brilliant your mind or strategy, if you're*
> *playing a solo game, you'll always lose out to a team."*
> —REID HOFFMAN

Consider the unlikely partnership between NASA and LEGO. A space agency and a toy company would seem to have different goals and different audiences, but a spark of awareness brought them together in 2010. NASA hoped to inspire a new generation of young people to become scientists and engineers; LEGO wanted to help children dream big and think creatively about their futures. NASA began the collaboration by putting a small LEGO shuttle toy aboard the *Discovery*, and allowing LEGO to use NASA branding on a set of kits based on the spacecraft. LEGO built a special website for kids about space exploration.

Then, in 2011, the program really took off (pun very much intended) when the space shuttle *Endeavor* carried eleven LEGO kits to the International Space Station. The models were used by scientists in space to conduct experiments, while earthbound kids and their teachers went along on the journey virtually; complementary curriculum allowed them to build their own models and interact with the astronauts. I imagine that one day we'll be hearing from astronauts who got their start building LEGO toys.

Earlier I described Airbnb as a Big Bet, but it's also an example of a company that has thrived thanks to unexpected partnerships. The first of these was with KLM Airlines in 2014. Realizing that their businesses intersected, the two companies decided to explore a partnership—but it's the way they approached their collaboration that's so interesting. To launch their collaboration, KLM converted an MD-11 jet into a faux Airbnb apartment, replacing rows of seats with a cool living room and a large, comfy bed. Then they ran a contest, offering three winners one night each on the jet. Contestants only had to write about why they deserved to win in one hundred words or less.

The contest was a huge success, with more than 3 million video views. The lucky winners got a dream Airbnb experience, and like the typical rental, the jet came with a list of rules, including "No flying," and "Please treat our plane like you'd treat your own plane." Today the two companies continue to cross-market. KLM passengers can book their Airbnb stays through KLM along with their flights. A spark of imagination, and a willingness to share resources and credit, created a lasting partnership.

Another great example of this principle is impact investing. Impact investments are defined as investments that represent both a financial and a social return, and they can span across all asset classes, sectors, and geographies. We've already highlighted the stories of a few such companies, such as Warby Parker, Happy Family, and Greyston Bakery, but they're just the tip of the iceberg when it comes to new enterprises formed with profit and purpose equally in mind.

In recent years, there has been dramatic growth in the number of companies, funds, and organizations created in support of the movement. A cottage industry of associations, conferences, research efforts, advisors, and platforms has generated a burgeoning ecosystem for the movement. Indeed, some of the world's hottest brands have arisen out of this trend, representing positive social impact through the very products and services they bring to market. A new class of investors and entrepreneurs are coming together with the simple, but somewhat radical, idea that social impacts have equal importance to financial returns.

In 2017, the amount of capital going into this new field more than doubled from the previous year to reach $228 billion. And traditional financial institutions have jumped in—from JPMorgan to TPG, from Goldman Sachs to Bain Capital. The world's largest pension fund, Japan's GPIF, allocated more than 1 trillion yen to socially responsible investments. Philanthropies and nonprofits are getting in the game as well, ranging from a $1 billion impact investing commitment from the Ford Foundation to a $50 million commitment from the National Geographic Society, with the belief that these investments can provide an attractive financial return while furthering the mission of these organizations.

• • •

One of my favorite examples of a most incongruous partnership came as the world was grappling with the Ebola crisis. Between March 2014 and March 2016, West Africa experienced the largest outbreak of Ebola in history. President Obama appointed our friend, colleague, and Case Foundation board member Ron Klain as the Ebola Czar. Aid workers and medical personnel rushed to help, but the dangers of infection were very real. Unfortunately, the hazmat suits used in the region were unwieldy, requiring thirty-one steps to put on, and twenty minutes and two people to remove. The fabric didn't breathe and the face masks fogged up within minutes. Even worse, the most common design had twenty-eight known points of potential contamination.

To start looking for solutions to this crisis, the global health

nonprofit Jhpiego and Johns Hopkins University announced a design challenge to create a better hazmat suit. And the challenge
brought in some unexpected players. Of course, there were engineering students, public health workers, and virologists in the
mix. But there was also a surprising candidate—a wedding dress
seamstress named Jill Andrews. Jill was fearless because she didn't
put herself in a box. As she put it, "It's all engineering. If you can
build a bra, you can build a bridge." She wasn't afraid to go beyond
her bubble and join the weekend hack-a-thon at Johns Hopkins.
And as is often the case, her fearlessness led to a great innovation.

Jill, along with a team from Johns Hopkins, created an Ebola
hazmat suit that was one piece, with a zipper down the back to
simplify removal. They also introduced a larger face mask and a
small battery-powered fan that blows air into the hood. In a field of
1,500 applicants, their design was declared a winner and received
a substantial USAID grant to work further to develop the suit.
But first, Jill got to take the Ebola suit to New York Fashion Week,
where Jhpiego partnered with the International Rescue Committee and the GE Foundation to present a pop-up lounge to display
her creation. Jill had always dreamed of having a dress at Fashion
Week, but she never could have imagined it would be a lifesaving
hazmat suit. It remains my hope that this kind of thinking will
inspire the next generation of protective suits for those caring for
Ebola victims, as others are drawn to innovate in this area.

As Jill proved, sometimes the answer you're seeking lies outside
your own network. By opening ourselves to unlikely collaborations, new problem-solving tools become available and challenges
that once seemed impossible become possible. Melinda Gates affirmed this truth in 2016 with a TED talk titled "What Nonprofits

Can Learn from Coca-Cola." Gates posed an intriguing question. "Coke is everywhere," she said. "In fact, when I travel to the developing world, Coke feels ubiquitous. And so, when I come back from these trips, and I'm thinking about development, and I'm flying home and I'm thinking, 'We're trying to deliver condoms to people or vaccinations' . . . Coke's success kind of stops [you] and makes you wonder: How is it that they can get Coke to these far-flung places? If they can do that, why can't governments and NGOs do the same thing?" And by partnering with Coke on Project Last Mile, delivering lifesaving vaccines to remote areas of Africa, the Gates Foundation and other partners were able to bridge the gaps that had previously been insurmountable.

> *"Change happens by listening and then starting a dialogue with the people who are doing something you don't believe is right."*
>
> —JANE GOODALL

One of the most meaningful examples of the power of unlikely partnerships in my own life occurred in 2003, during George W. Bush's administration, when I was invited to join a small gathering in the Roosevelt Room of the White House to discuss the HIV/AIDS pandemic, which had by that time killed more than 20 million of the 60 million who were infected in Africa, leaving behind 14 million orphans. By bringing together private sector and faith-based leaders, President Bush set out to gain support for an ambitious new program, which would involve a three-point solution similar to one that had been effectively tried in Uganda. It was known as ABC: A = promoting abstinence, B = monogamy (be faithful), C = use condoms.

It was not an easy gathering. On the right, there was concern about promoting condoms, especially from Catholic leaders who opposed birth control; on the left, there was resistance to funds going to prevention efforts rather than treatment, with a particular disdain for abstinence counseling, which was seen as moralistic and ineffective. Further complicating the matter was tension about the so-called Mexico City Policy first enacted under President Reagan to block federal funding of NGOs that provide abortion counseling or services. Here again, the right and the left were at odds over whether to extend this policy and refuse to fund organizations that were providing much-needed HIV/AIDS services throughout Africa.

Our group in the Roosevelt Room brought strongly held views on both sides. There were leaders from the US Catholic Church, Randall Tobias, CEO of the pharmaceuticals firm Eli Lilly, and Chuck Colson, who'd founded the faith-based Prison Fellowship following his own prison sentence stemming from illegal activities in the Nixon White House. He represented the Christian Right. There was also Kate Carr, CEO of the Elizabeth Glaser Pediatric AIDS Foundation, one of the most prominent AIDS organizations, whose founder had contracted the disease as a result of a blood transfusion during childbirth. The daughter she bore died of AIDS, and Elizabeth Glaser herself succumbed to the disease only a few years later. In addition, key staff from the White House were in attendance, including my good friend Josh Bolton, who would later become chief of staff to George W. Bush.

How on earth could such a mixed group reach consensus? At first, it seemed impossible. Not only did those gathered represent extreme differences in perspective, but few had ever been in the same room together. A stranger walking into that room could have cut the tension with a knife. And yet, even through the tensions, the urgent need to do *something* kept everyone in the conversation.

Still, we were at an impasse. Then someone uttered words that stopped everyone in their tracks: "People are dying even as we speak. Women, children, and a generation of young men in Africa are being taken from us at an alarming rate. This has to stop. We can't leave this room without a commitment to work together and find a way forward." These words were met by a long silence as the gravity of the moment set in. The mood in the room shifted. Slowly, the conversation tilted to what might be possible. Before the close of the meeting, there were concrete steps put forth, with a strong sense that there were no winners and losers, but rather compassionate, committed individuals who were willing to collaborate, even if it meant they didn't get everything they wanted.

Later, I joined the others to watch President Bush sign the President's Emergency Plan for AIDS Relief (PEPFAR), a $15 billion commitment that included both prevention efforts and treatment. The program likely would not have made it through Congress without the willingness of those on both sides to signal their support. In 2017, the rock star Bono visited President Bush at his ranch in Texas to thank him for the role of PEPFAR in fighting HIV/AIDS.

In an interview, Bono observed the electric effect of unlikely collaborations in winning support from politicians on different sides of the aisle. "The administration isn't afraid of rock stars and student activists—they are used to us," he said. "But they are nervous of soccer moms and church folk. Now, when soccer moms and church folk start hanging around with rock stars and activists, then they really start paying attention."

Bono's insight and the other stories in this chapter hit home. Sometimes to be seen and heard, you have to bring along a totally unexpected ally. In an era when so many people are retreating to their corners, the fearless changemakers have to walk out into the center of the arena and beckon all the others to join them.

EIGHTEEN

BE BETTER TOGETHER

In my late twenties, when I started at AOL, I was one of two women on the executive team. It was an incredible group of highly talented individuals who came together weekly to talk about our various responsibilities and to help guide the company. As I discuss in other parts of this book, I tried to bring confidence to my role as a leader in the company, but always knew I lacked many of the credentials of my peers. Some had run their own companies, had received numerous accolades, or held graduate degrees. Others had decades of experience that I did not.

We generally had strong mutual respect and the dynamic was positive, but during a particularly difficult period the relationships within the executive committee frayed somewhat and tensions rose. A consultant was called in to work with us. As part of the process, the consultant asked us to complete a Myers–Briggs assessment, a tool often used in teamwork to highlight personality types. The test groups people into sixteen types based on their answers. One category measures if you are "thinking" or "feeling." As we set out to take the test, we joked that in our technology company, we hoped we had mostly "thinking" types. And not surprisingly, the team all scored as "thinking"—except for one person . . . *me.*

As you can imagine, I was mortified, and I got plenty of teasing from the others. But then something happened that left a lasting impression. The consultant explained that "feeling" doesn't mean you are not "thinking," and "thinking" does not mean you aren't "feeling." Those designations merely suggest whether someone tends to make decisions through logic or through considering people. Then she told us that the strongest teams have both, and that if we were *all* the same, we wouldn't have the benefit of a broad perspective in decision making. She then asked each of us to talk about the benefit of our differences—how we had seen our differences play out and add value. We had been through some tough layoffs, and some around the table mentioned how grateful they were that I could see impacts on people and the culture that helped to shape our actions and bring more dignity to the situation. I, in turn, pointed out how I benefited from more of a purely analytical view in some decisions we had to make. That exercise transformed the way our team worked together. There was a new trust and an understanding that, despite our differences, we were "better together."

To change the way we interact with the world, we have to change the way we *see* each other. I love Lin-Manuel Miranda's *Hamilton* because it accomplishes this so radically. What could be more familiar than our picture of the founding fathers as sober, aging white men? Lin-Manuel turned this well-established narrative on its head in his daring hip-hop musical, with a multiracial cast portraying those iconic characters. The focus of the story is Alexander Hamilton, the nation's first secretary of the Treasury—in itself, an unlikely topic for public fascination.

In creating *Hamilton,* Lin-Manuel wasn't trying to be outrageous. But when he read Ron Chernow's eight-hundred-page *Alexander Hamilton,* he found himself seeing Hamilton for the first time as an immigrant with guts and brilliance who fought his way to the top. When he previewed one of the show's songs at the White House, he told the audience he thought Hamilton embodied hip-hop, and everyone laughed. But he meant it—and after his performance of the musical's now-famous opening number, others saw it too.

Hamilton has changed the cultural landscape, making it no longer unexpected to see men like Washington, Jefferson, and Hamilton portrayed as nonwhite. And after I saw *Hamilton* on Broadway, I found myself thinking about what a gift it is to live in an age and country of such rich diversity and inclusion.

• • •

As discussed earlier, the 2015 *Diversity Matters* report from McKinsey showed that diversity makes companies more productive and prosperous. When they expanded the research in 2018 under the name *Delivering Through Diversity,* McKinsey found that many companies saw inclusion and diversity as a competitive advantage and, specifically, as an enabler of growth. Looking at a thousand companies across twelve countries, McKinsey found that the trend continued with a direct correlation between gender and ethnic diversity and profitability, with companies that lacked diversity being penalized, underperforming their peers by 27 percent.

The importance of diversity—or the act of bringing together people with different perspectives and backgrounds—is getting the attention of the nation's largest companies, whose portfolios now commonly highlight their efforts. When Deloitte reported on its studies of diversity and inclusion in the workplace, it found that organizations with inclusive cultures were two times more likely to meet or exceed financial targets, six times more likely to be innovative and agile, and eight times more likely to achieve better business outcomes. And in 2018, *Forbes* published its first list of the best employers for diversity. The number-one company was perhaps unexpected: Northern Trust, a Chicago-based investment management firm with 17,800 employees. Thirty-eight percent of top executives were women, and the board was 23 percent African American.

> *"The giant computer that is our unconscious silently crunches all the data it can from the experiences we've had, the people we've met, the lessons we've learned, the books we've read, the movies we've seen, and so on, and it forms an opinion."*
> —MALCOLM GLADWELL

Applauding companies that lead the way on diversity forces more widespread change. But since there is a growing consensus that diversity matters, why are we seeing so many businesses lagging behind? Research shows that women and people of color disproportionately lack access to the capital, support, and networking that young companies need to grow. By failing to give all aspiring entrepreneurs the same advantages, we may very well be stifling the creators of the next great innovations.

The numbers are stark: In recent years, only 10 percent of venture capital–backed companies have had a female founder. Less than 1 percent of these companies have an African American founder. And 75 percent of all venture capital went to just three states—California, New York, and Massachusetts—leaving the rest of the country to compete for just a quarter of the pie. And yet those forty-seven underfunded states have produced hundreds of Fortune 500 firms, proving that great companies can be built anywhere.

Current data suggest that the fastest-growing segment of entrepreneurs are women, followed closely by African Americans and Hispanics. Female-owned firms are growing at 1.5 times the national average, while African American–owned firms are growing at a rate of 60 percent. (Non-minority-owned businesses are growing at a rate of just 9 percent.) And there is a lot of evidence that these businesses often outperform their counterparts. One venture capital firm found that the female-led start-ups it funded performed 63 percent better than those with all-male founding teams. Good thing, then, that there are more than 9 million such companies today.

We have the opportunity to energize our economy by expanding our reach when it comes to investing in promising new companies. And perhaps the first step is to change what we think success looks like. Only a couple of years ago, I was in a meeting at the Case Foundation when someone suggested we do a Google Image search using the phrase "successful entrepreneur." We found ourselves staring at a page full of pictures of young white men. No women. No people of color. Not one. It wasn't as if these were all images of famous entrepreneurs either. Some of them were stock photos. That was the day we decided to share the stories of all entrepreneurs from *all* backgrounds to get the message out that great entrepreneurs come from all places, genders, races, and backgrounds.

To begin opening the door to more people, we must first acknowledge that unconscious bias is real—for you and for me. Why does this matter? Because there is a growing awareness that the sameness we're seeing in who gets venture capital funding might have a lot to do with unconscious bias, especially since 93 percent of investing partners at the top 100 venture firms are men—and predominantly white men. How comfortable will entrepreneurs who aren't male or white be during pitches when there isn't anyone like them at the table? Can an all-white panel of investors really understand the potential value of new innovations by and for people unlike them?

We must laud venture capitalists who add inclusiveness to their standard criteria for assessing potential investments. In some ways, this is just common sense, but it also makes good business sense. Women make the majority of consumer purchases, so if an investor is considering a new product, wouldn't it help to get the perspective of someone who better represents the potential market?

There are a growing number of leaders calling on all of us to embrace a world of more inclusion. One of them is my dear friend Mellody Hobson, the African American president of Ariel Investments, the largest minority-owned investment firm in the world. To break through our automatic biases, Mellody suggests that we be "color-brave" instead of color-blind—which is to say, intentional about inviting people to the table who don't look or live like we do. She puts her firm's investment resources behind these principles, staying away from companies that lack diversity in their leadership and boardrooms. And Ariel itself is a model of diversity: 51 percent of its staff is female, 27 percent African American, and 20 percent Asian and Hispanic.

Mellody is a remarkable woman—brilliant, kind, tough, and amazingly accomplished. (A few years back, when the term "girl crush" first came into parlance, I asked my daughters what it meant. They laughed and explained it to me. Then a few weeks later I met Mellody and understood.) But even Mellody has encountered bias out in the world. She tells a story in a TED talk of a time in 2006 when she was helping her friend Harold Ford, also African American, run for the Senate. She called a woman she knew who worked for a major New York media company and convinced her to set up an editorial luncheon for Ford. "And we get to the receptionist, and we say, 'We're here for the lunch,'" she said. "She motions for us to follow her. We walk through a series of corridors, and all of a sudden we find ourselves in a stark room, at which point she looks at us and she says, 'Where are your uniforms?' Just as this happens, my friend rushes in. The blood drains from her face. There are literally no words, right? And I look at her, and I say, 'Now, don't you think we need more than one black person in the US Senate?'"

• • •

American ingenuity has brought us the quality of life we enjoy today. If we seize this opportunity to democratize entrepreneurship and build more inclusive businesses, we will strengthen our economy and make sure that anyone from anywhere has a fair shot at the American dream. That means being fearless in disrupting the status quo—not just in business but all across our culture.

The great conductor Zubin Mehta once said there was no place for women in orchestras. Fortunately, not everyone agreed. In the 1950s, the Boston Symphony Orchestra was the first to hit on the idea of holding auditions with the performers behind a curtain. Unable to see the musicians, judges based their choices solely on talent. Other orchestras followed suit, and most orchestras do blind auditions today. Not surprisingly, researchers have found that blind auditions in the first round of tryouts improve a woman's likelihood of advancing to later rounds by 50 percent. When blind auditions are held in all rounds, the likelihood of a woman being chosen triples. Today women sit in more than 50 percent of all orchestra chairs.

> *"A baseball team entirely composed of catchers could have high esprit de corps. But it would not perform very well on the field."*
> —SARA ELLISON, MIT

As a woman—and one who started out in the male-dominated tech industry—I am intimately familiar with the challenges we face to get a seat at the table. So I'm always especially interested in stories of fearless women.

When I came across the story of Dame Stephanie Shirley, an early software distribution pioneer in the UK, I wondered how I had never heard of her. Shirley, who was born in Vienna, was part of the Kindertransport program that saved nearly 100,000 Jewish children from the Nazis by sending them to England without their parents. She was five years old. "I'm only alive because so long ago, I was helped by generous strangers," she said of her experience.

From an early age, her ambition was clear: "To make my life one that was worth saving." With a passion for mathematics, which was not taught at her all-girls school, she received authorization to take math classes at a neighboring boys' school. Then, despite not having a college degree, she set out to have a career, starting at London's Post Office Research Station, where she built computers from scratch and wrote code. Her interest in technology grew, and for six years she took classes at night, earning an honors degree in mathematics.

In 1959, Shirley started her own software company, Freelance Programmers, predominantly employing women—many of whom had left the industry when they got married, or when they had children. (She was also a visionary in allowing employees to work from home.) Her initial start-up capital was six British pounds, equal to about seventeen dollars at the time. She grew the company's value into the hundreds of millions, and when she retired at age sixty, she became a philanthropist. Along the way she adopted the name Steve to help her in the male-dominated field. Now in her eighties, Shirley still has a keen sense of humor. "You can always tell ambitious women by the shape of our heads," she says. "They're flat on top for being patted patronizingly. And we have larger feet to stand away from the kitchen sink."

Another one of my favorite stories involves a woman named Vernice Armour, nicknamed FlyGirl. Vernice was the first African American female naval aviator in the Marine Corps and the first African American female combat pilot in the US Armed Forces. In flight school, she finished number one in a class of two hundred. She flew the AH-1W SuperCobra attack helicopter in the 2003 invasion of Iraq, and served two tours during Operation Iraqi Freedom. But Vernice was racking up firsts even before she joined the Marines. In civilian life, she was a Nashville police officer and the first African American woman on the motorcycle squad. Following her service, Vernice launched VAI Consulting and Training to encourage others to find their own breakthroughs.

In 2016, I was invited by the Harvard Business School Alumni Association to lead a discussion for Women's History Month with Barbara Hackman Franklin, herself a graduate of Harvard Business School in 1964, the first class to include women. Franklin is a remarkable person who was instrumental in opening up presidential appointments for women. Surprisingly, she did so at the invitation of President Richard Nixon.

When we think of great champions for women throughout history, chances are Richard Nixon would not be on most people's lists. But in August 1972, *Newsweek* declared that "the person in Washington who has done the most for the women's movement may be Richard Nixon." Due to the Watergate scandal and his subsequent resignation, President Nixon is rarely given credit for advancing the role of women in government. Nor is the appropriate acknowledgment given to women like Franklin, who played a crucial part in his efforts.

Here's how it happened. In early 1969, Nixon had been in office only a month when, at a press conference, a hand shot up from the third row. It belonged to a reporter named Vera Glaser, whose question would reverberate far beyond the room. "Mr. President," she said, "you have so far made about two hundred high-level cabinet and other policy position appointments, and of these, only three have gone to women. Can you tell us, sir, whether we can expect a more equitable recognition of women's ability, or are we going to remain a lost sex?"

There was some laughter, but the president grew serious. "I had not known that only three had gone to women," he said, "and I shall see that we correct that imbalance very promptly."

Barbara Hackman Franklin, who was on the corporate planning

staff of the First National City Bank (later Citibank), was tapped to come to Washington to lead the new White House Women Recruiting Program. Thanks in no small part to Franklin's efforts, the number of women in top-level positions tripled after just one year, and more than a thousand women were hired or promoted at a time when personnel cuts shrank the federal government by 5 percent. Many of these women would remain in public service for decades, including Elizabeth Hanford Dole, who served a seven-year term on the Federal Trade Commission and was later elected US senator from North Carolina, and Assistant Attorney General Carla Hills, who later became secretary of housing and urban development to President Gerald Ford and US trade representative under President George H. W. Bush.

There's a common assumption that as the number of women in high-level jobs increases, this trajectory will continue upward. But that's not a given. There can be a two-steps-forward, one-step-back character to the fight for equality. As of this writing, women hold only 19 percent of seats in Congress, a number that has remained relatively stagnant in recent years, although more women than ever are running in upcoming elections. And while President Barack Obama's cabinet was the most diverse in history, President Donald Trump's is the least diverse in thirty years.

But it's good to remember that sometimes a breakthrough can happen when a single woman raises her voice high enough to set things in motion. Change happens when people think of diversity not just as a nice thing to have but, as data have revealed, as a smart strategy to maximize performance.

NINETEEN

LEVERAGE PARTNERSHIPS FOR GROWTH

The technology sector I entered in my early twenties seemed at times like the Wild West. We had no road maps to guide us. We were just an odd collection of players counting on each other to survive.

Following the advent of the microprocessor in 1971, personal computers were mainly built by geeks who enjoyed tinkering and who would purchase kits to put together their own crude machines. By the 1980s, when I entered the tech world, things had evolved somewhat. But still, providing a compelling online experience (by the standards of those days) required a complicated and expensive shopping list of devices, including:

- a desktop or personal computer, ranging in price from $595 for the then-trendy Commodore 64, to as much as $2,495 for the first Macintosh;
- a display screen (not always standard in those days);
- software (early personal computers didn't necessarily have a built-in hard drive or storage);
- a modem;
- a subscription to an online service.

One thing we knew for sure back then: we all needed each other. Software without a computer was useless. A computer without compelling applications had no value. An online service could not connect without a modem. You get the idea. What this meant for the growth of the industry was not only that partnerships had to be formed, but that we needed to create networks to accelerate our progress, improve our operations, and continue to innovate. For these reasons, collaboration was the hallmark of the early personal computer and online marketplace, perhaps much more so than today. We dreamed big dreams of a connected world with communication and content at one's fingertips.

My title in those early days was manager of joint marketing. It was my job to travel across the country to visit computer companies, software companies, modem companies, and telephone companies to strike partnership agreements wherein the hardware and software companies would bundle and promote a subscription to an online service—hopefully mine.

Later, as I advanced in my career and landed at AOL, we expanded our unlikely partnerships. Omaha Steaks bundled AOL software with their famous steaks, and NASCAR featured an AOL racing car and gave away software at their events. There were unexpected alliances for content too: quilters across America had a very active quilting forum, Lucasfilm partnered to produce one of the earliest interactive games online, and *Time* magazine partnered with AOL for our first-ever national online conference on Billy Graham's seventy-fifth birthday.

One of the most enduring lessons from AOL came from our ability to leverage our competition through partnerships and alliances. That's right—our competition! In the mid-1990s, Microsoft was a tremendous threat to AOL. Because its operating system dominated the market, it could greatly influence the success of anything Microsoft bundled on the home screen—and the potential failure of those left out of a bundle. As news spread that Microsoft was developing its own online service, to be bundled with Windows 95, we at AOL grew concerned. We knew Microsoft could use its market power to demand that computer manufacturers promote its new online service exclusively, shutting out AOL. To make a long story short, we prevailed in getting AOL bundled by agreeing to use Microsoft's browser for AOL member access to the Internet. It became a co-bundle—two competitors promoting each other's products.

Similarly, when it finally became legal for consumers to access the Internet in 1993 (yes, before that it was only legal for academia, government, and scientific organizations to connect to the Internet), AOL went to work building bridges to the World Wide Web. Among the first things we introduced was a search engine that enabled members to surf the Web while on the AOL service. Then we discovered a new upstart called Google that was providing its own search engine directly to consumers. We knew we had to act. So a deal was struck to make Google the official AOL search engine. In return, AOL got a 5 percent equity stake and a share of revenues generated. Here again, instead of putting our energy into fighting the power of a competitor, we "joined" them. The result was a better search experience for our customers, and a windfall when Google later went public.

Some might look at more recent history and suggest that AOL reached a little too far beyond its bubble in the merger with Time Warner in 2000, which ended in failure. My own perspective is that it was the right partnership strategy, but the wrong blend of teams. Business partnerships, like most relationships, come down to people. In the case of AOL/Time Warner, both sides dug in their heels when it came to blending cultures. There's a well-known saying, often attributed to Peter Drucker, that "culture eats strategy for breakfast." When reaching beyond your bubble, take note of the people and the culture you'll be working with when assessing opportunities.

Today revolutions in technology have brought about fundamental shifts in the way people think, form groups, and do their work. The Monitor Institute, which works with social impact organizations, calls this new way "working wikily," meaning working with greater openness, transparency, decentralized decision making, and collective action fueled by social media.

• • •

When you're planning a project or movement, it's important to examine a spectrum of potential allies to avoid relying on the "usual suspects." Sometimes it helps to draw a series of circles. In the bull's-eye should be those potential partners that share the most common interests or markets. Work out from the inner circle to assess who else might have a strategic interest in the area you're targeting.

In the civil rights movement, for example, Reverend Martin Luther King Jr. and his contemporaries started by mobilizing southern blacks before shifting to bringing northern whites over to their cause. When Harvey Milk began the LGBT movement in San Francisco, he started reaching out to the gay community on Castro Street, but then expanded to include straight liberals in the

San Francisco Bay area. Colonel John Boyd, the military reformer who helped change the way the Pentagon functions, pursued a similar path, first preparing briefings on the proposed changes for junior officers, then congressional staffers, then elected officials, and finally the top generals.

When examining who out there might help to accelerate your efforts, consider who could be important allies, or even foot soldiers. And think about incorporating not-so-obvious partners into the process. Take a lesson from Liberia. A decade of civil war left the country's health infrastructure devastated. There were just fifty doctors to care for a population of 4 million, and care was almost completely unavailable in rural areas, where people died from normally treatable conditions, such as a difficult childbirth. HIV was a growing crisis too. So a group of Liberian civil war survivors and American health workers joined forces in 2007, with Peter Luckow at the helm. Their project, called Tiyatien Health, began Liberia's first rural, public HIV program with just $6,000 in seed money. They changed the name to Last Mile Health in 2013, in reference to those areas most in need, Liberia's "last mile."

Alone, Last Mile Health might have continued to struggle to meet even a small portion of rural communities' needs. But then the Ebola crisis struck, and with it came an idea that enabled the nonprofit to reach beyond its bubble and scale its efforts at the same time. Last Mile Health tapped an unlikely source of health workers—people in the affected communities. With access to Liberian Health Ministry funds, Last Mile Health set out to train and equip 1,300 health workers in thirty-eight clinics across southeastern Liberia. Now, with a committed government partner and an army of community health workers, the program has an opportunity to aid rural areas that were for too long considered, according to the organization's mission statement, "too difficult to reach and too expensive to serve."

> *"It takes two flints to make a fire."*
> —LOUISA MAY ALCOTT

This is the wonderful secret of successful collaboration: using "two flints" to spark opportunities with benefits for all. John Doerr, in telling the story of the founding of Google in his book *Measure What Matters*, describes the company's cofounders, Sergey Brin and Larry Page, in this way: "Sergey was exuberant, mercurial, strongly opinionated and able to leap intellectual chasms in a single bound. A Soviet-born immigrant, he was a canny, creative negotiator and a principled leader. Sergey was restless, always pushing for more; he might drop to the floor in the middle of a meeting for a set of pushups. Larry was an engineer's engineer, the son of a computer science pioneer. He was a soft-spoken nonconformist, a rebel with a 10x cause to make the Internet exponentially more relevant. While Sergey crafted the commerce of technology, Larry toiled on the product and imagined the impossible. He was a blue-sky thinker with his feet on the ground." So while you might see a picture of the Google cofounders side by side and assume they're just two white guys, this misses their differences, which together made Google one of the most transformative companies in America today. It's no coincidence that two so dissimilar people built this outlier of a company.

We know that when individual powerhouses join forces, the result can be dramatic, which is why it can be so painful to see our political leaders retreat into partisanship. And it can be especially inspiring, not to mention effective, when leaders cross party lines for the greater good.

In late 2004, after an earthquake and tsunami devastated eleven nations in Southeast Asia, President George W. Bush enlisted two former presidents—his father, George H. W. Bush, and Bill Clinton—to raise funds for the recovery effort. Not only were the two from different parties, but their rivalry was personal. Clinton had defeated the elder Bush in 1992, denying him a second term in office. George W. Bush had defeated Clinton's vice president, Al Gore, in 2000. But on their trip to Asia, the former presidents became so close that George W. Bush later came to refer to Clinton as "my brother from another mother." Their visit to Asia made a huge emotional impact, and they raised millions in aid. The joint mission was so effective that in 2010, President Obama sent Clinton and George W. Bush on a similar mission to Haiti after a devastating earthquake.

The data are overwhelming: we are better together. But should this really come as a surprise? Now the challenge for each one of us is to ask, "Who isn't at the table?" or "What unique perspectives could help us avoid blind spots or widen our aperture?" as we look for new opportunities to seize.

TWENTY

NOW GO, GET OUTSIDE YOUR BUBBLE . . . EVERY DAY

We all have unconscious biases and blind spots that skew the way we view the world. These biases impact our daily lives in countless ways, often placing us on the outside looking in—and not always understanding what we see. The only way to overcome these blind spots is to make a deliberate effort to see and experience what we don't know. And as Stephen R. Covey recommends in *The 7 Habits of Highly Effective People*, seek first to understand, then to be understood.

As my husband and I have discovered on our trips across America, when you travel an unfamiliar road, you'll see things you didn't know were there. Sounds obvious, right? But knowing and doing are different things.

As you launch your Big Bet, you'll need to surround yourself with people different from yourself, remembering that diverse teams that bring an array of backgrounds and perspectives outperform. So where to begin? Make a list of your team's attributes. What's missing? How can you complement the knowledge, experience, and skills you already have? If you are just getting started, make sure you set aside time on your calendar for coffee or lunch with those who might bring a fresh perspective to your efforts. Organizations can form advisory groups, add personnel, or hire consultants to fill in the gaps. Don't be afraid to hear points of view that make you uncomfortable.

Be intentional in planning your alliances. Think about the interests or markets you serve, and then make a list of which other organizations share those interests. Some will be obvious, while others might be less apparent, like the rock star and the president, or National Geographic and 21st Century Fox.

Like Jill Andrews, we can step outside our comfort zones to offer a solution never imagined by those on the inside. Like the collaborators behind PEPFAR, we can give up a little in order to achieve a larger good. Like Mellody Hobson, we can pioneer diversity to build a stronger economy. Like AOL, we can partner with our competitors. Like George H. W. Bush and Bill Clinton, we can shrug off old antagonisms to change the world.

What first step will you take to reach beyond your bubble today?

PART FIVE

LET URGENCY
CONQUER FEAR

Seize the moment

Be a first responder

Don't overthink or overanalyze. Do.

Now go, be the one

TWENTY-ONE

SEIZE THE MOMENT

We can choose to act with urgency, or have urgency thrust upon us. But there's a reason someone coined the phrase "a crisis is a terrible thing to waste." When your back is against the wall, when options are limited, when time is not on your side, a certain clarity can set in, bringing with it a boldness you might not have known you had in you. Soldiers find extraordinary bravery in the heat of battle, everyday citizens perform acts of heroism during disasters, and people accomplish unimaginable feats when they're running out of time. They might not be wholly aware of the risks, or be able to calculate their impact. They just act.

Many of the stories highlighted in earlier chapters had an element of urgency. Barbara Van Dahlen knew our veterans need better mental health care; Ernest Shackleton, abandoned to the most ferocious of conditions in Antarctica, knew he and his crew faced death if he didn't act. But crises are not always so extreme. Brian Chesky and Joe Gebbia felt the urgency of a looming rent payment, with no money in the bank. The founders of Warby Parker needed to quickly and inexpensively replace a pair of glasses.

How individuals and companies act in times of crisis can be a true measure of their fearlessness. Nearly every large company has a "crisis management" strategy, but when a corporate crisis becomes a real emergency, it is courage, not management, that is remembered.

One of the iconic stories of corporate courage began in September 1982, when four people in Chicago died after taking Tylenol capsules that had been laced with potassium cyanide. Without hesitation, Johnson & Johnson CEO James E. Burke pulled all Tylenol off the shelves and launched a public campaign warning people not to buy the product. (No one at Johnson & Johnson knew who had poisoned the pills, and the perpetrator was never found.) Pulling Tylenol out of circulation cost millions of dollars, and Tylenol's market share plummeted from 38 percent to 8 percent. Yet the company's *only* consideration was saving lives. And there's little doubt that its fast action did just that. In the long run, Burke also saved the product. There was some pressure within the company to discontinue Tylenol and relaunch the product under a new name. But Burke refused. Instead, he reintroduced Tylenol encased in new tamper-resistant packaging in a corporate commitment to safety that eased public fears. The industry followed his lead, making products tamper-resistant and safer for consumers. Within a year, market share was restored, and Johnson & Johnson became a model of crisis management.

> *"I learned that courage was not the absence of fear, but the triumph over it."*
> —NELSON MANDELA

My own lessons in corporate courage and the value of a crisis came relatively early in my career. In the early days at the start-up that would become America Online, before we introduced the AOL service, the company spent more than a year developing an online service with Apple, known as AppleLink, that bore the Apple logo. Our young start-up burned considerable time and resources in creating the software and back-end technologies. However, from the start of the relationship, there was trouble. Apple had never grown comfortable with the idea of another company operating a product/service under its name, much less a fledgling start-up. Then one morning, the dreaded call came—Apple was canceling our deal.

In his book *The Third Wave*, my husband recalls receiving that call. "It was like going through the five stages of grief all in the same afternoon," he wrote. We considered our limited options to save the company. In the end, we decided to take the technology we'd built and use it to launch our own online service. "We need to create our own brand, propelled by our own marketing, paid for by us," Steve said at the time. But where would the money to do this come from now that the Apple deal was dead? After a series of conversations with Apple executives, we arrived at a termination settlement of $3 million. Today that wouldn't be enough to keep many young companies alive, but it worked then.

I recall the lightness of that moment. Yes, there was some fear as we stepped out on our own. But freed from our troubled relationship with Apple, we saw a new sense of energy and enthusiasm set in. I found myself actually looking forward to the possibilities each day might bring. By that time it was my job to lead the communications, marketing, and branding efforts to build scale for this new service. Once we landed on a name—America Online—our mantra became to "get America online." We knew the clock was ticking—we had limited funds, and a product to get out the door. So we coalesced around this mission, seizing the moment and letting urgency conquer any remaining fear.

> *"Life is either a daring adventure or nothing."*
> —HELEN KELLER

While corporate crises can teach us about the power of letting urgency conquer fear, so too can stories of brave men and women who lived through trying times—rare moments that set apart those who face down their fears and do something extraordinary.

Earlier in the book, I mentioned my German grandparents, for whom I have enormous respect. When they left their homeland in the 1920s, an ugly movement was beginning to take shape there. The Nazi Party would soon come to power, exploiting the fears of those living in an economy that was left in ruins after World War I. As a child, when I began to learn the history of Germany, I would often pepper my grandparents with questions: Could they help me understand the rise of the Nazi Party? Could they explain the inaction of citizens who saw the threat but did not find a way to stop it? How was it possible that so many remained mute while their fellow citizens were carted off to camps or shot in the streets? My grandparents had no answers. They too struggled with the same questions about what had become of their former homeland.

Perhaps because of my family ties to Germany, I became fascinated with the stories of ordinary people who stepped in to shelter those in need, or to do their part in the resistance movement. I was especially drawn to stories of those who risked their lives to harbor and protect Jews during the war. I began reading many accounts of bravery and sacrifice from that period. In one of these books, *The Hiding Place*, I was inspired by the story of the author, Corrie ten Boom.

Corrie ten Boom was an unmarried woman in her early fifties living with her father and sister at the start of the war. (Perhaps because I was a young teen when I first heard her story, I could not believe that so unlikely a character could emerge to play such a historic and heroic role.) Corrie's fearless role in the resistance began without forethought in an instant of daring; she seized the moment. One morning, working in the family's watchmaking shop (she was Holland's first female watchmaker), Corrie heard a commotion across the street. Looking out her window, she saw a Jewish neighbor being held at gunpoint by Nazi officials, who were pushing him out into the street. The soldiers then ran back into his shop and began destroying its contents. Corrie rushed from her workbench out to her neighbor, who had been left unguarded and in a daze. Corrie grabbed his arm and hastily led him through her shop and upstairs to her apartment.

This instinctive gesture began Corrie's dual life. She appeared to be a kindly spinster, but behind the scenes she was a soldier of the resistance. Corrie arranged for a sophisticated hiding place to be built behind one of the walls of her bedroom, large enough to hold half a dozen refugees. And she built a network that helped the people she hid find a way out of Amsterdam. Through her efforts, hundreds of Jews were saved.

Corrie's secret activities continued throughout the war, until one day in February 1944. She was sick in bed with the flu when the house was raided. Miraculously, soldiers did not discover the hiding place. But Corrie, her father, and her sister, Betsie, were arrested. They were first sent to a nearby prison that housed political prisoners. Frail and elderly, Corrie's father did not survive the harsh conditions. After his death, Corrie and Betsie were sent to the notorious Ravensbrück concentration camp, where disease, starvation, and exhaustion from heavy manual labor were routine. But Corrie and her weakening sister did what they could to serve those even worse off than themselves. At night, fellow prisoners would gather around as Betsie read words of hope from a smuggled Bible that Corrie had carried with her throughout their ordeal. Betsie did not survive, dying in December 1944. Days after her death, Corrie was unexpectedly released. She returned home to Amsterdam and reestablished a connection with the resistance network, continuing her work until the Allied army retook Holland in May 1945.

I was fifteen when I read Corrie's story, and I devoured the book. Soon after, I learned that *The Hiding Place* had been made into a film, and that Corrie was coming in person to a local theater to speak at the film's opening. I couldn't believe it—and of course I went. I was near tears as Corrie, then in her eighties, with silver hair swept up in a bun, came to the podium. The audience sat enraptured as she spoke. Even in writing this, I recall very clearly how moving and inspiring her words were. At the close of the film, I was able to meet Corrie—something I will never forget. She had an inner beauty that shone through like a beacon of love. But her kind and gentle manner belied a strength and fearlessness that helped make her the hero she was to so many.

• • •

As for those questions I asked my grandparents back in the day, I think we all knew the answer, even if it went unspoken. And we know the answer now. Fear created the silence. Fear created the inaction. Fear created the appearance of complacency.

Like Corrie, and like so many of the fearless changemakers we have highlighted, we often face a choice in moments when urgency beckons. We can look away and let complacency take hold, or we can use these moments and let urgency conquer fear to make a difference.

In 1963, standing on the steps of the Lincoln Memorial, Reverend Martin Luther King Jr. spoke of the "fierce urgency of now" in the struggle to end segregation. "This is no time to engage in the luxury of cooling off or to take the tranquilizing drug of gradualism," he said, important words we should all embrace.

TWENTY-TWO

BE A FIRST RESPONDER

As a nation, we've come to rely on trained first responders in times of crisis. But what if those we rely on to act fail to do so? Sometimes an unlikely first responder rushes in to fill the void.

Walmart has often been criticized for the ways its empire has overwhelmed mom-and-pop stores on America's Main Streets. As one of the nation's largest corporations, with annual revenue of hundreds of billions of dollars, Walmart and its power had attracted some resentment. Then a devastating hurricane showed what Walmart was really made of.

Hurricane Katrina struck southern Louisiana and Mississippi on August 29, 2005, leaving large portions of New Orleans underwater. Nearly two thousand people died, and thousands more were stranded on rooftops and in makeshift shelters. Those who made it to the Superdome sports arena, where emergency shelter was offered, found deplorable conditions and inadequate food and water.

FEMA—the Federal Emergency Management Agency, the official first responder for natural disasters—downplayed the crisis and imperiously rejected offers of help from across the nation. Days ticked by, and Americans watched with disbelief as the desperate scene played out on national news.

Walmart CEO H. Lee Scott Jr. knew that his company, which had hundreds of stores throughout the region, could help. Not only did Walmart put enormous resources into relief efforts—including 2,500 truckloads of merchandise—but Scott also deputized Walmart workers in the region to make decisions about what would best help their communities. Scott sent out this instruction to store managers: "A lot of you are going to have to make decisions above your level. Make the best decision that you can with the information that's available to you at the time, and, above all, do the right thing."

In one story of initiative and daring, Jessica Lewis, the assistant manager of a store in Waveland, Mississippi, drove a bulldozer through the ruins of the store, collecting dry food, clothing, water, and other resources to give to neighbors. "She didn't call the home office and ask for permission," Scott said admiringly. "She just did the right thing. Just like thousands of our associates who also did the right thing, a trait I am proud to say is bred in our culture."

After the storm, Scott challenged his board and top executives to reflect on Walmart's ability to achieve social good. "What if," he asked, "we used our size and resources to make this country and this earth an even better place for all of us: customers, associates, our children, and generations unborn? What would that mean? Could we do it? Is this consistent with our business model? What if the very things that many people criticize us for—our size and reach—became a trusted friend and ally to all, just as it did in Katrina?"

> *"I have been impressed with the urgency of doing. Knowing is not enough. We must apply. Being willing is not enough. We must do."*
>
> —LEONARDO DA VINCI

Any company—or any person—is capable of stepping into the center of a crisis and making a difference. That's certainly what a celebrity chef from Washington, DC, believes.

José Andrés calls himself a product of the "new American dream." He arrived in the United States from Spain at age twenty, eager to develop his talents as a chef and to use his craft to make a difference beyond the kitchen. In the early 1990s he was offered the position of chef at Jaleo, a new tapas restaurant in DC that quickly became a favorite spot for Washingtonians. As his reputation spread, he and his business partner, Rob Wilder, opened several other restaurants around the city.

I first met José about fifteen years ago when he hosted a fund-raising event for DC Central Kitchen, an organization that works to combat hunger in Washington. (José served on the board.) I took note of his drive and his frenetic style—seamlessly going from a conversation about the power of food to change the world to refilling empty wineglasses he spotted in guests' hands.

José's commitment to making a difference has led him to become a somewhat unlikely first responder. In 2010, he founded the World Central Kitchen after traveling to Haiti following the devastating earthquake. "We cooked meals for people and showed them what could be done with the power of the sun," he said. In the years since, he has continued to provide disaster relief, most recently in the aftermath of natural disasters, such as those that befell Houston, Puerto Rico, and Guatemala. He views food as both important nourishment and as an agent for change. Upon arriving, José sets up a makeshift kitchen and, oftentimes in sweltering heat, begins a daily pattern of cooking and preparing food, which he videotapes for social media to raise awareness and funds. (He's careful to provide public thanks to the corporate and nonprofit partners who help him mobilize.) The *Washington Post* has called José "the face of American disaster relief."

José's work in Puerto Rico was extraordinary. After Hurricane Maria hit, wiping out power and causing massive food and water shortages, José arrived on the island and immediately mobilized an army of chefs, companies, and citizens from all walks of life to feed the population. The goal was to get on the ground quickly and provide meals to as many people as possible. Scaling rapidly, from one kitchen serving 1,000 meals on the first day to twenty-three kitchens serving 175,000 meals in one day, José and his teams became the lifeline for many on the island. In the end, they served more than 3.5 million meals. The *New York Times* called World Central Kitchen "the largest emergency feeding program ever set up by a group of chefs."

The same year that José founded World Central Kitchen, Secretary of State Hillary Clinton also named him a Culinary Ambassador of the Global Alliance for Clean Cookstoves. It's estimated that as many as 3 billion people around the world cook their food or heat their homes with wood fires that are not properly contained. The smoke from these fires can lead to health problems ranging from infections to heart and lung disease, and even death. The fires' toll on the planet is also significant, leading to deforestation and significant carbon release into the atmosphere.

José also played an active role in Michelle Obama's Let's Move campaign, which emphasizes the need for fruits and vegetables in a healthy diet, opening a new fast-casual vegetarian restaurant, ironically called Beefsteak, with the tagline "Vegetables Unleashed." Throughout this period, he has used his platform (he was named one of *Time* magazine's 100 Most Influential People in the World in 2012 and again in 2018) to push against calls to further restrict the flow of immigrants into the United States.

With all his success, José remains humble. "My name is José Andrés, and I am a cook," he said as he stood in the shadow of the Washington Monument in 2014 to deliver a commencement address to graduates of George Washington University. "When President Knapp asked me to speak at your commencement, I thought, why a chef? Even my daughters said, 'They asked you to speak or to cook lunch for graduates?'" The students laughed, charmed by this man who was anything but a simple cook.

José spoke to the graduates about the new American dream, advising, "It's not about having high-paying jobs, big houses, fast cars. There is nothing wrong with that, but the new American dream is bigger. It's about how to achieve your success while also making an impact in the world. What you create for yourselves you must also create for others."

José embodies the kind of fearless spirit we regularly witness when our nation experiences a crisis. Think of the volunteers who mobilized in 2017 as California's fires raged, including two young women, Emily Putt and Hilary Hansen, who rescued 150 horses left behind when their owners were forced to flee. Think of small-business owners like Houston's Jim McIngvale, known as Mattress Mack, who opened his mattress stores to provide shelter to hundreds of people forced out of their homes when Hurricane Harvey hit in 2017. Think of concertgoer Jonathan Smith, who helped others escape America's deadliest mass shooting in modern history, at a country music festival in Las Vegas, before he was shot twice himself. (Doctors left one of the bullets in his neck, fearful that removing it would do more damage.) Day by day, across our nation and around the world, the fearless, selfless acts of those among us can inspire hope—and perhaps the courage to act—in us as well.

• • •

Paul Rieckhoff never planned for his life to go the way it did. After graduation from Amherst, he headed for Wall Street. "For a while I was worried that my generation was going to be a generation where nothing important happened," he told students in an address at his alma mater. "There was no call for us to answer." Then 9/11 happened. Paul, who was in the National Guard as a "weekend warrior," volunteered for the army and was sent to Iraq, where he served until 2004. He came home to a nation ill-equipped to serve this new generation of vets. Veterans of Iraq and Afghanistan soon came to realize they didn't have an advocate to champion their unique needs and concerns.

While he was visiting Amherst, dressed in his military uniform, two Vietnam veterans Paul had never before met walked up to him on the street. "Welcome home, man," they said. "Now we need you to serve again." That was his inspiration for the creation of Iraq and Afghanistan Veterans of America (IAVA).

For a long time, Paul felt like a voice in the wilderness. He recognized that while we as a nation are full of patriotic spirit in supporting soldiers when they march off to fight, we often lose interest when they return home with wounds and PTSD only to struggle rejoining the job market. Since its founding more than a dozen years ago, IAVA has become one of the most influential organizations championing support for veterans, with nearly half a million veteran members today. Paul's mission is to bring the urgency felt on the battlefield back home, and his game-changing efforts have resulted in job programs, mental health resources, mentorship programs, and community-building initiatives.

It was the urgency of September 11 that originally caused Paul to shift gears and answer a call. Today it is the urgency of the plight of men and women who have selflessly served our nation that drives him forward. Knowing Paul, my bet is he won't rest until the mission is accomplished.

It's easy to think of first responders as bold and brash, people perhaps more brave than we see ourselves. The stories in this chapter teach us that anyone from anywhere can be a first responder to a crisis they witness. Is there an immediate or even ongoing crisis you are observing that is calling you to jump in and respond with action?

TWENTY-THREE

DON'T OVERTHINK OR OVERANALYZE. DO.

Much has been written about the difference between people who act with urgency and those who procrastinate. Perhaps Nike's famous "Just Do It" slogan has a secondary message: "Don't spend too much time thinking about it." This would seem to contradict advice most of us have received along the way. Think of how many times you've heard, "Don't be hasty!" or "Think this through carefully." It's no wonder that "Just Do It" doesn't come naturally.

I realized there was value in both of these messages the first time I stood high in the air preparing to bungee jump. My brain was ordering me, "Don't do it," perhaps rightfully so. We *want* our brains to tell us not to take risks that could endanger us. But I had carefully considered the risk I was taking, and was convinced I would be safe. And so, counting down, "Three . . . two . . .one," I jumped. That was nearly thirty years ago, and of course, it all worked out.

In her book *The 5 Second Rule*, Mel Robbins suggests that the "countdown approach" is a great "brain hack" to get things started if you're feeling fear or stress or the urge to procrastinate. In the book's opening, Robbins describes a period in her life when she couldn't find the motivation to get out of bed. One morning, having watched a rocket launch the previous day, she found herself counting out loud—"Five . . . four . . . three . . . two . . . one"—and vaulted out of bed. For Robbins, this moment was life-changing. In an interview with *Inc.* magazine, she describes the countdown approach this way: "When you act with courage, your brain is not involved. Your heart speaks first, and you listen. . . . The five seconds is critical in both triggering the fast-acting part of your brain as well as limiting the influence of the slow-acting part of your brain. Decide and act." Once triggered, she said, you can use the next five minutes to focus on whatever you're fearful of doing. "As long as you make that five-second decision to commit five minutes, you will have broken the cycle and proven that you can confront the stress."

In their book *Fail Fast, Fail Often*, authors Ryan Babineaux and John Krumboltz reflect on a series of research studies in a segment entitled "Too Much Thinking Can Stop You in Your Tracks." In summarizing the studies' findings, they conclude that "the more time you spend collecting information and making choices:

- the more confused and hesitant you will become;
- the more likely you will be to stick with the status quo and ignore better options;
- the more likely you will be to allow trivial factors to bias your behavior;
- the less energy you will have to take action and persevere in the face of challenges."

This is intriguing data, and it might help to alleviate some stress for people who have no choice but to act *now*, as was the case during one of our nation's worst financial crises. At the end of 2008, with the economy in free fall, General Motors was on the verge of collapse; by the end of the year, GM was more than $30 billion in debt. At the end of his administration, President George W. Bush approved a short-term $17 billion bailout, which would keep the lights on but not solve the crisis.

In February 2009, with a new administration in the White House, GM chairman Rick Wagoner came to Washington to meet with President Obama's auto task force and beg for help. Insolvency would mean not only the loss of tens of thousands of jobs at companies like General Motors and Chrysler, but also at their suppliers. But a bailout wasn't popular with Congress. Many believed GM was a victim of its own poor management, and that as a private company, it should bear the consequences of its choices.

Faced with having to make a fast decision, President Obama and his economic advisors decided to make a Big Bet and approve an $85 billion bailout of GM and Chrysler. There was no way to know if this would pointlessly drain public coffers or revitalize the auto industry. But the risk of not acting was devastating, so urgency conquered fear.

And it worked. President Obama and Treasury Secretary Timothy Geithner's willingness to act bolstered the economy and saved one of America's leading industries. But as Geithner notes: "You can't judge a decision by how it turns out, only by whether it made sense given the information available at the time."

This same spirit of urgency was present in another fearless effort undertaken by President Obama and his team. Concerned about opportunity gaps facing boys and young men of color, and with a goal of assuring that all youth have the opportunity to reach their full potential, President Obama announced the creation of My

Brother's Keeper, an initiative that galvanized the public, private, and nonprofit sectors to work on these issues. The initiative led to the creation of the MBK Alliance, launched in 2015 to scale and sustain this mission. In late 2017, MBK Alliance became an initiative of the Obama Foundation. The Case Foundation's very own Michael Smith was first tapped to help lead this effort from the White House and today serves as the executive director of the MBK Alliance. (Michael played an important role in helping us to develop our original Be Fearless work and in spreading its message.) He is uniquely suited to lead MBK Alliance, having overcome significant odds himself as a young man growing up in challenging circumstances. He's a true innovator, and anyone who knows him sees how he lives with a sense of urgency in addressing issues in our communities, and how he brings a fearless spirit to his work every day.

It's easy enough to see how "Just Do It" thinking can come more naturally in the heat of the moment, but there are countless stories of people one step removed from crises who still find a way to jump in with urgency to make a difference.

In 1954, Bertha and Harry Holt—she a nurse, he a farmer and lumberjack—sat in disbelief in a high school auditorium in Oregon as they listened to a talk by Dr. Bob Pierce, a young pastor who had recently founded a new relief organization, World Vision. As United Nations forces, most of them American, withdrew from the Korean Peninsula following the Korean War, many children born to Korean mothers and fathered by soldiers were abandoned. Dr. Pierce showed a heart-wrenching film about these homeless children, who were considered outcasts by their society because of their supposed "mixed blood."

The Holts, who were in their fifties, had known struggles of their own in the Great Depression, having left a failed farm in the Midwest to build a successful sawmill business in Oregon. When a heart attack left him in a wheelchair in 1950, Harry sold the business and began rebuilding his strength. Grateful for his recovery, Harry told Bertha he wanted to spend the days ahead showing his appreciation for God's goodness to him.

Moved by the images of abandoned Korean children on the screen, the Holts began sending donations to World Vision. But they couldn't get the desperate children out of their minds. So with six children of their own, some of whom still lived at home, they decided to adopt eight Korean children. But when they tried to arrange the paperwork, they were thwarted by a law that limited foreign adoptions to one child per family. Told it would require an act of Congress to change the law, Bertha replied, "Then that's what we'll do."

While Harry left for Korea to begin arranging adoptions, Bertha launched a lobbying campaign in Congress. The so-called Holt Law was signed in 1955, and the Holts added eight children—newborns and toddlers—to their family. But their efforts didn't end there. By the following year, the Holts were running an adoption agency out of a Salvation Army building to help bring more children to America and to aid in domestic adoption. But they found that children with disabilities or special needs could not easily find homes. So in late 1961, they broke ground on a residential facility in Seoul, financed by the sale of their sawmill business. Harry died suddenly not long after, but Bertha launched the effort and she found success, continuing until her death in 2000. She was known in Korea as Grandma Holt.

> "A small body of determined spirits fired by an unquenchable
> faith in their mission can alter the course of history."
>
> —MAHATMA GANDHI

In 2017, I visited the compound in Seoul, together with a close friend—a Holt adoptee herself. The facility is now run by the Holts' daughter Molly, who is eighty. I was especially moved by the Holt Agency Museum, a tribute to the founders and their work, located on the property. The entry wall of the museum displays thousands of tiny images of orphans adopted over time. The collage of these photos forms three words: "Love in Action." We strolled the halls filled with memorabilia, stories, and documentation of tens of thousands of lives that were changed because of the caring, compassionate commitment of a humble couple from Eugene, Oregon. They did more than take action; they started a movement.

• • •

Marta Gabre-Tsadick has spent decades working to improve the lives of the people of Ethiopia. Together with her husband, Deme Tekle-Wold, she founded Project Mercy, a nonprofit organization providing food, education, job training, and health care for Ethiopians and refugees from other African nations. When Steve and I first visited Marta in 2004, the urgency was a growing famine that was sweeping across the country. I'd learned about Marta from my friend Billy Shore, cofounder of Share Our Strength, who had been raising funds in the US to aid the efforts on the ground in Ethiopia, and we had joined in the effort. I told Billy that I wanted to better understand the challenges and opportunities in Ethiopia, and he had two words for me: "Just go." So we did.

I can still remember the bumpy four-hour car ride spent dodging cattle and goats along a crowded dirt road as we made our way out to the remote village of Yetebon. When we finally stepped out of the dust-covered truck, I was immediately struck by Marta's gentle spirit and a beauty that seemed to glow from within as she greeted us.

We were also intrigued by her long and impressive history of engagement. Marta was already married with two children when she left Ethiopia to attend college in the United States, returning home in 1954 to serve as director of Ethiopia's Ministry for Foreign Affairs under the famed Emperor Haile Selassie. She later became the nation's first female senator. But when civil war broke out in 1974 and the emperor was placed under house arrest by the new Communist regime, Marta, Deme, and their children were forced to flee, as their own lives were at risk. After months of uncertainty living as refugees in Greece, they were allowed to enter the United States, thanks to the generous sponsorship of a community in Fort Wayne, Indiana, where, slowly, they began to rebuild their lives. Ever mindful of those they'd left behind, they founded Project Mercy.

In the early 1990s, Ethiopia's Communist government was toppled, and Marta and Deme returned to their homeland to expand Project Mercy's work. They built a compound that would grow through the years to include a school, a job training center, a hospital, and an orphanage. In 2013, members of the US House and Senate and the director of the United States Agency for International Development (USAID) came to Project

Mercy to see firsthand the important work taking place. Later, announcing a four-year, $2 million commitment to expand Project Mercy's health-care services and nutrition programs, USAID director Rajiv Shah lauded Marta's "holistic program that doesn't treat individuals as beneficiaries but rather as real partners in the development of vibrant communities in Ethiopia. All you have to do," he continued, "is meet people like Marta and Deme to know that the future of development lies in their hands, not ours."

The mission of Project Mercy is not just about providing food during a famine or addressing each crisis as it comes. "In order to fight against poverty, you have to attack it from many different directions and then pluck it out," Marta has said. "We cannot educate children if the only outcome is to make them discontented with the limited job opportunities currently available to them. We cannot just treat symptoms of malnutrition in the clinic and not also improve nutrition and agricultural production. We cannot teach good hygiene practices if people still need to bathe and drink from the same contaminated water supply. Clean water piped into each home is possible only if economic conditions are improved for the entire community."

People like Harry and Bertha Holt and Marta and Deme model lives lived with urgency, even if the commitment stretches over decades or generations. And over the years, their actions coalesced into something even bigger than simple philanthropy. They became movement-building.

"One thing that movements do is come up with ways to make the important urgent," Marshall Ganz, a senior lecturer at Harvard Kennedy School, has noted. He was talking about climate change, which, while surely urgent, has effects that reveal themselves slowly over time and as a result can be less obvious to some.

One of the lessons he draws from his decades working in and studying social movements is that only moral urgency can move individuals to act. This deeply felt passion for justice and action is often accompanied by hope, or the sense of possibility. "If you look at the core of any social movement, there are highly committed people who are ready to take risks," he says. "It's not just about passing a law—at heart they are movements of moral reform."

In the dark of night, each of us may wonder, "Would I have the courage to step up and act when the time comes?" Yet moments of urgency don't just occur when storm troopers arrive at the door.

In 1910, after serving eight years as president, Theodore Roosevelt gave a groundbreaking speech about the tension between those who criticize and complain and those who jump in, against the odds and in spite of fear. "It is not the critic who counts; not the man who points out how the strong man stumbles, or where the doer of deeds could have done them better," he said. "The credit belongs to the man who is actually in the arena, whose face is marred by dust and sweat and blood; who strives valiantly; who errs, who comes short again and again, because there is no effort without error and shortcoming; but who does actually strive to do the deeds; who knows great enthusiasms, the great devotions; who spends himself in a worthy cause; who at the best knows in the end the triumph of high achievement, and who at the worst, if he fails, at least fails while daring greatly, so that his place shall never be with those cold and timid souls who neither know victory nor defeat." Roosevelt may have spoken of "the man," but today his call goes out to all who hear the whisper or the shout and are inspired.

Noted professor, author, and speaker Brené Brown was thinking of Roosevelt's call when she wrote *Daring Greatly: How the Courage to Be Vulnerable Transforms the Way We Live, Love, Parent, and Lead*. Brown, who often focuses on the crippling effects of shame and fear, believes that daring greatly requires setting aside self-doubt and refusing to allow uncertainty to give you pause. She writes, "When we spend our lives waiting until we're perfect or bulletproof before we walk into the arena, we ultimately sacrifice relationships and opportunities that may not be recoverable, we squander our precious time, and we turn our backs on our gifts, our unique contributions that only we can make."

As the stories in this chapter demonstrate, urgency can be a powerful motivator to fearlessly get in the arena. Is there something in your life that is so important it can become an urgent call to act? Consider Marta, threatened and removed from her homeland. Rather than run away or cower, she instead acted with urgency to help create a better future for others. The Holts knew young lives hung in the balance in Korea and jumped in to make a difference for all time. Teddy Roosevelt's famous speech reminds us that despite difficulties, despite failures and shortcomings, we can all make the choice to strive valiantly. It is up to each one of us to let the urgency of the moment conquer our fears and drive us forward.

TWENTY-FOUR

NOW GO, BE THE ONE

"We are what we choose," Jeff Bezos told Princeton University students in a 2010 commencement address that was all about the importance of choosing to act. When I read this address, I realized he was talking about letting urgency conquer fear. And the most striking part was when Jeff asked a series of pointed questions that challenged the graduates to think deeply about the most important choices they would make for their lives. Let me share some of them with you:

> How will you use your gifts? What choices will you make?
>
> Will inertia be your guide, or will you follow your passions?
>
> Will you follow dogma, or will you be original?
>
> Will you choose a life of ease, or a life of service and adventure?
>
> When it's tough, will you give up, or will you be relentless?

These are fitting questions for college graduates, but I share them here because they are also the kind of questions anyone who aspires to live a life of purpose should ask—and answer. The first step to greatness is deciding to be the one who doesn't just let life happen to you.

Each of us is responsible for the kind of impact we have on the world. If you're reading this book, I suspect that you have a deep desire to strike out—rejecting the ordinary and making a difference. So pick your arena. You can make change through business, through the arts, through education, through a social movement, through politics, in your neighborhood. It's up to you which trail you blaze.

> *"Never doubt that a small group of thoughtful people could change the world. Indeed, it's the only thing that ever has."*
> —MARGARET MEAD

In his book *The Excellence Dividend*, management consultant Tom Peters describes how traditional organizations too often rely on careful, studied analysis before making a move, whereas young organizations excel through urgent action. "There was no grand plan," he writes. "There was no plan at all. The starting point was the STARTING." So start. Take the path Peters describes as "WTTMSW—whoever tries the most stuff wins."

As John Kotter of Harvard Business School points out, nobody wants to admit they're complacent. People are busy. If you ask them, they'll cite many ways they're engaged. What we're talking about here is different. It takes some bravado. Ask yourself: Can you stand in the shoes of people like Corrie ten Boom? Can you, like Walmart's Jessica Lewis, get on that bulldozer and bust into the rubble to find supplies? Can you adopt the spirit of Oprah or Astro Teller and let failure teach you? Can you align your daily business with a larger mission, as chef José Andrés has? Can you, like the Holts, see a need and figure out, without overthinking, how you personally can help?

Can you imagine saying out loud:

- *I'm the one who will find a solution to this problem.*
- *I'm the one who will show up when there's an emergency.*
- *I'm the one who will take the big risk when the company needs a spark.*
- *I'm the one who will care for the person who's left behind.*
- *I'm the one who will speak up when others are silent.*
- *I'm the one who will tell the story that needs to be told.*
- *I'm the one, with my heart in my throat, who will dare to act.*

Can you decide to be the one? Here's the secret: it doesn't take a remarkable ability, great charisma, or any special advantages. People become heroes not because they are blessed with extraordinary powers, but because when they see the urgency, they simply choose to act.

The time is now for all of us to decide whether we will hold back or plunge into lives of meaning. It is my sincere hope that you will feel that urgency as an inner force and choose to be among those who step forward. That voice calling is meant for you.

EPILOGUE

ON RETURNING TO NORMAL

They say when one door closes, another one opens, but the saying is usually used figuratively. In this case, when the airplane door closed in Washington, DC, it wasn't long before another one opened in a small town in the nation's heartland, seemingly worlds away.

It was my husband's idea that I travel alone to the town where I was raised to begin writing this book. He couldn't have known that along the way, I would fall in love. Not with some new person, of course, but with the town that raised me, the town that instilled in me the values that form the basis of who I am, the town that in so many ways shaped me, even though circumstance didn't allow me to stay beyond adolescence.

I returned to Normal to ask big questions and seek big answers. I no longer have any family there, except for those whose graves I visited, but the Airbnb home I rented just around the corner from the house where my grandparents once lived assured that I would not run from my past. I rented a bike for my breaks from writing, and every day I would pass the home of my grandparents and offer a knowing nod. I never did knock on the door to introduce myself

to the new owners. It was enough to just be near a place that held
so many cherished memories.

The home in which I stayed was more than a hundred years old
and lovingly restored. It wasn't lost on me that I was dwelling in
a structure whose own past had been so thoroughly explored. The
foundations of the home were solid, carrying the structure through
a century of change. Its best and most defining attributes—the
wavy glass, the rich mahogany wood, the bowed patio overlooking the generous, tree-lined backyard—were unchanged at their
core, but carefully restored to bring back their original glory. In the
silence of the evenings, or in the early-morning light, one could
almost hear echoes of the family that first occupied the home in
the early 1900s.

In the quiet of my solitude, I reflected that we have foundations
too, set at birth, and special attributes to nurture and protect, lest
they be scratched or worn down over time. As children, we rush to
climb high trees, to try new things without much thought to our
own limitations. When we fall, we get back up and keep going. For
me, this was life in Normal. But this type of fearless living is not
"normal" at all.

So the question becomes, how do we each dig deep inside ourselves to find our own path back, perhaps not to normal, but to
that early, more fearless self who whispered, "I dare you"?

I wrote this book because in the six years I've been sharing the
Be Fearless principles, I've had countless men and women come
back to tell me how the principles inspired them. A young MBA
student from Notre Dame changed his career focus to public engagement. A woman who had for decades thought about hatching
a plan for a new museum in her town is now well on the way to

making that happen. Such stories come back to me often, from companies, nonprofits, entrepreneurs, social activists, and everyday people who have been inspired to be bold, take risks, make failure matter, and march toward their dreams to make a difference in the world. Maybe one day I'll hear one from you.

Now go, change the world.

AFTERWORD: ON THE ROAD WITH
BE FEARLESS

Since the publication of the hardcover of *Be Fearless* in January 2019, I've had the privilege of once again traveling across the United States and to other countries to share the principles and inspiring stories included in the book. And I am happy to report that people from all places and walks of life are embracing the idea of being fearless—pushing past their fears to make important changes in their lives, their organizations, and their communities. By going on the road with *Be Fearless*, I was able to listen, learn, and be inspired by the tens of thousands who have come to our book events and who have reached out to share stories of their own fearless journeys.

With more than one hundred audiences and counting, they have taught me that my book is only the opening of a longer conversation that people are eager to have.

In a time of great anxiety and rapid change, I find that people everywhere are looking for inspiration and a framework to help them see how they can make a difference. I've seen how the *Be Fearless* principles serve as a starting point for those asking, "What can I do right now?"

One thing became clear right out of the gate: no matter the audience or the setting, people wanted to talk about how powerful a force both fear and failure can be in keeping individuals and organizations from pursuing big bets—and how much they wanted to overcome them.

I should have anticipated this response because I'd seen it when I sent drafts of the book's manuscript to a variety of leaders for review and comment. One senior executive from a top private sector firm in New York City—a person anyone would consider at the pinnacle of a successful career—wrote me a deeply personal note to tell me that reading the book helped him realize something very profound: He had sometimes resisted moving forward with transformative ideas at his firm because he feared failure. And he hadn't really appreciated it until he read the book. He'd settled into his "comfort zone" of success and stopped challenging himself and his teams. Recognizing it, he promised to change.

More recently, as I came offstage at an event at National Geographic, one of our young Explorers told me when she was first asked to speak at the event, she demurred. She was gripped by fear. Yet serendipitously, the invitation had come as she was reading *Be Fearless*. She told me the book made her realize it was fear that was keeping her from the important spotlight opportunity. After reading the book, she agreed to speak. As she spoke from the stage, I saw how deeply moved and inspired the audience was, and the applause was enthusiastic and genuine. The message she delivered that day, and the work she shared with us, was important, and I would hate to think the moment might have been lost due to the sometimes-paralyzing power of fear.

But the truth is, at times I actually don't even need to hear words from people to understand how individuals and organizations can become gripped with fear and how even the smallest failure can make a person or a team become gun-shy as they think about future risk-taking. Whether it is a small roundtable or an audience of more than a thousand people, I see the discomfort in the eyes and in the body language of those gathered when I talk about the principles of Making Failure Matter or Be Bold, Take Risks. When it comes time for the Q&A, the questions are all about strategies to help move past fear. In response, I always encourage people to take the power away from fear or failure by simply putting it on the table and talking about it. Whether they are at the outset of a new endeavor, challenging themselves to pursue a big bet, revising their plan in the face of a setback, or making an adjustment in midcourse to respond to changes in the marketplace, talking about failure at the outset can be key: What could go wrong? How can you stage your efforts to minimize the impacts of failures if they happen along the way? What kind of support can you expect if you encounter failure? Think it through, work with it. Don't let fear or failure stop you in your fearless endeavors.

As I've shared the evidence from our research and experience underscoring that it is ordinary people who do extraordinary things, I've seen eyes light up. I've recognized the moment when, suddenly, some of those gathered embrace the idea—"It really can be me!"

It's amazing what can happen when companies aren't limited by old biases and leaders are open to ideas from the unlikeliest of sources. A powerful example of this can be found in the story of Richard Montañez, and if I had known it when I set out to write *Be Fearless*, it definitely would have been included in the hardcover.

A Mexican immigrant, Montañez grew up in the small farming community of Guasti, California. There his mother, father, and grandfather raised him and his ten siblings in a one-room adobe structure, making a meager living picking grapes and working the fields under the hot California sun. Montañez didn't speak English and struggled to keep up in school, ultimately leaving after the fourth grade, never having learned to read or to write. He was happy at age eighteen to find a janitorial job at Frito-Lay. His skills were limited, but his imagination and commitment to learning were boundless. As he studied Frito-Lay's product line, he realized there were no spicy or hot snacks like the ones that his friends often sought. Wanting to introduce his community to Cheetos, he tested out a new recipe on his family and friends, mixing in hot spices and offering samples. His recipe was so well received that he decided to make a bold move: he called the office of then CEO Roger Enrico to invite him to try the product. "I didn't know the rules," he would later say when asked how he'd had the nerve to go straight to the CEO. But Enrico was impressed with the young janitor and agreed to visit the plant a few weeks later. Together with a cadre of executives, Enrico listened as Montañez—sporting a new three-dollar tie he had bought for the occasion—laid out his ideas before they tasted the spicy Cheetos he'd produced. At the end of the meeting, Enrico was reported to have said, "Put your mop away. You're coming with us." Frito-Lay tested Flamin' Hot Cheetos in East LA and the pilot was so successful that the brand eventually went global, becoming a multi-billion-dollar product line for Frito-Lay. Montañez has enjoyed a thirty-five-year career with PepsiCo (the holding company for Frito-Lay) and now serves as VP of Multicultural Sales and Community Activation.

Montañez's story is a great example of Reach Beyond Your Bubble in action. Enrico (who was a dear personal friend of mine and a fellow trustee at the National Geographic Society before his passing in 2016) was reaching far beyond his bubble as he embraced the young janitor with a limited education and limited reading and writing skills. But the bet paid off both for Montañez and for Frito-Lay as a new and robust market emerged for their products.

I'm always looking for ways to reach beyond my own bubble. In *Be Fearless* I've described how my husband, Steve, and I take summer RV excursions to out-of-the-way places that are less familiar to us, and where we know that people are likely to bring different perspectives. In this way, we stretch ourselves to connect with people and parts of the country we would not otherwise know or perhaps not fully understand. As I write this, we are preparing for our next adventure—a five-week RV road trip across the country and back. I can't wait to see what we will discover along the way.

One of the most exciting things about being on the road for the book tour has been seeing how deeply people feel the urgency of this moment and how committed they are to engaging to find real solutions in their neighborhoods, in their towns, and in their lives. It's clear we live in divided times, not just in the United States, but across the globe. Time and again I have seen a true desire to overcome the paralysis that can set in when life is overwhelming and problems seem too hard to solve. That burning impatience or agitation to find a better way forward is universal, and I have witnessed it wherever I travel. In words and action, people are saying that we need a more fearless America and a more fearless world where more individuals and institutions allow urgency to push them to boldly embrace new ideas and solutions. It is not a time for bystanders. We need all the ideas and all the players on the field to build the bright future we hope for.

I've discovered that this sense of urgency can reach down and influence even the youngest citizens. I was touched a few weeks after the book was published when a young mother reached out to let me know she and her eight-year-old daughter had listened to the audio version of the book together. She said that as they listened to the book, they shared ideas about how they could make sure they could use their talents to make a difference in this world.

Young people today are choosing to be fearless in countless ways, which is why I value the time I spend on college campuses. I included many of them on my book tour. At the University of Maryland's Smith School of Business, before I spoke to a broader audience, I was delighted to sit down with a dozen female undergraduate and graduate students who are building new companies or new nonprofits while earning their business degrees. These young women—all of them first-generation college students, and most of them immigrants—shared stories of fearlessness and perseverance that have stayed with me as I am reminded of how easy it is to talk about being fearless, yet how hard it is for some to live out the principles in challenging circumstances. I walked away inspired, and was truly delighted when the Smith School of Business made *Be Fearless* part of its summer reading list for students.

While personal stories always capture our attention, it is also important to applaud when larger organizations embrace fearlessness. In many cases, as large organizations find success, it becomes difficult to leave the comfort zone to forge new ways forward or to foster innovations that might be needed in a fast changing world. Whenever I think about established institutions and their boards facing fearless decisions, I am reminded of an important moment at National Geographic more than one hundred years ago that was vividly described to me by our archivist. At the time, the editor of *National Geographic* magazine made what was then a radical and risky decision: to put photographs in the magazine. At the time, photography was a "new tech" that was viewed by many as an unserious and passing fad. So, when the matter was taken up by the Board of Trustees, there was skepticism about whether photography was befitting of a serious science and exploration journal. The editor described how photos could be used to help bring the stories to life and expand the magazine's appeal, but some trustees simply weren't having it. In the end, the board supported the use of photography in the magazine, but two board members eventually resigned over the decision!

Of course, in the ensuing century, *National Geographic* became known for the iconic images capturing the front lines of the unknown, both on our planet and out in the universe. And in 2019, that bold decision made more than one hundred years ago continues to enable the National Geographic brand to reach further and achieve new milestones, with National Geographic becoming the first global brand in the world to pass 100 million Instagram followers, and the film *Free Solo* winning an Oscar.

This venerable institution, which I am so proud to be a part of, continues to be bold and take risks in a wide variety of ways. To update a story that was featured in the book, in early 2019 National Geographic embraced a partnership with the Walt Disney Company (resulting from its acquisition of 21st Century Fox) that holds all the commercial businesses of National Geographic. The same fearless spirit that has been in the DNA of National Geographic for

131 years is alive as ever and encourages us to be vigilant for new opportunities to illuminate science, exploration, and storytelling for people everywhere.

One of the other joys of the days on the road sharing *Be Fearless* was the new ideas and perspectives I gained from readers of the book. One young woman who is a budding entrepreneur came up to me to praise the chapter entitled "Crash and Learn"—and then she told me about her way of expressing the same idea: "Win Some, Learn Some," which I loved! She has applied this thinking as she has confronted some early failures in the building of her new company.

Audiences everywhere have enjoyed hearing the story from the book about José Andrés's efforts in Puerto Rico and around the world to bring food security to communities following natural disasters. Following the publication of the book, Steve and I were privileged to join José in Puerto Rico where we saw firsthand the remarkable work he has continued to do there, after serving nearly four million of the victims of Hurricane Maria immediately following the crisis. Today, José and his team at World Central Kitchen are working to transform the island so that it can be more sustainable and self-sufficient and, therefore, more resilient when disaster strikes. Many readers have told me how energized they were by reading José's story. But here's the thing about José—and it's an important lesson on fearlessness. José didn't just do one thing, as important as it was. He keeps growing his sense of urgency. Since I wrote about his efforts, he has crossed the globe and has continued to work tirelessly and urgently when disasters and crises threaten food security. From the cyclone in Mozambique and earthquakes in Indonesia, to the hurricanes in Florida and the food crisis in

Venezuela, José has been on the ground taking risks and boldly creating solutions. For his efforts, and since the publication of *Be Fearless*, José was nominated for a Nobel Peace Prize.

And, along the way on the tour, I was especially pleased to find connections back to Madame C. J. Walker, whose remarkable life story I told in the very first chapter. Madame Walker's fearless journey played out more than a hundred years ago and while telling her story on book tour in Washington, DC, I was deeply moved to have with us her great-great-granddaughter and her biographer, A'Lelia Bundles. Separately, while I was addressing a large gathering at Indiana University in Indianapolis, a woman introduced herself whose grandmother had been among the three thousand women who worked at Madam C. J. Walker Manufacturing Company in that city more than a century ago.

Coming full circle, I was also honored to spend time while on tour with some of the key people featured in the book whose fearless and inspiring stories truly made the book possible. It has been deeply moving to see how people embrace their stories and to feel their love and support in the many months and many places I traveled to tell *Be Fearless* stories over the last year.

Among the highlights of the year, however, was a special moment I had with Jane Goodall, whose foreword touched so many. The setting was the United Nations in New York, where I had the true privilege of bestowing the *Forbes* 400 Lifetime Achievement Award to Jane for her more than sixty years of fearless changemaking. During our time together, I was struck by her lifelong commitment to making the world a better place for all species of our planet, and how even at age eighty-five, she carries a strong sense of urgency that keeps her on the road more than three hundred days a year.

Finally, 2019 marked the fiftieth anniversary celebration of the moonshot and Apollo 11's moon landing. While this might be among the most iconic Big Bets (as described in the book), the anniversary reminded us of the risks, the failures, the role of urgency, and the importance of staying the course even in the face of detractors—as there were many throughout the years leading up to the launch. The feat was so improbable that fifty years later we still marvel at the accomplishment. In many ways, the ethos of that special moment in American history, and the principles of fearlessness that were applied, are most clearly expressed by Apollo 11 astronaut Buzz Aldrin, who is now eighty-nine. I leave you with his words:

> *"Some people don't like to admit that they have failed or that they have not yet achieved their goals or lived up to their own expectations. But failure is not a sign of weakness. It is a sign that you are alive and growing. Get out of your comfort zone and be willing to take some risks as you work on new tasks. Some individuals have an aversion to risks, but it is not foolish to accept a level of risk, as long as the magnitude and worthiness of the goal you are seeking to achieve is commensurate with your risk. As your comfort zone expands, seek out even greater challenges. It is often said and it really is true: you can do almost anything if you put your mind to it."*
>
> —BUZZ ALDRIN

I hope you'll take inspiration from and heed these words as you embark on your own fearless journey into the future.

ACKNOWLEDGMENTS

The decision to write a book, and the process to get it done, varies for each author. For those writing their first book, once the manuscript is complete, there can be a tendency to approach the acknowledgments with a broader lens that includes people in life beyond those who specifically contributed in one way or another to the book itself. Such is the case here as I reflect on those central characters whose influence and inspiration brought me to this incredible moment where I sit poised to publish my own first book, in addition to those who have played a central role in bringing the Be Fearless principles to life with us over the last six years. Some of these individuals I've written about in the preceding pages and I've highlighted their stories, while the names of others appear here for the first time.

My husband, Steve, provided the earliest encouragement for this book. He was taken with the Be Fearless principles when I first shared the original research with him, and he saw the potential power of encouraging this entrepreneurial thinking across sectors and to people of all backgrounds. When Steve saw how the Be Fearless message resonated, he suggested I think about writing a book to more broadly convey this work. Steve is the Chairman of the Case Foundation, and although we are cofounders together, I credit Steve for his generous contributions to our work and to the scale of financial resources we have brought, as well as for providing his incredibly valuable insights as we've taken forward our philanthropic efforts over the last twenty-one years. He is a remarkable leader and brilliant innovator I continue to learn from and grow with, and I count myself blessed to have him as a life partner. Much as he does in the everyday life we share, in the writing of this book Steve encouraged me, challenged me, and expressed his loving support of the effort at each stage. There is no question I am more fearless in my life because of Steve.

Our blended family is comprised of five millennial-generation kids—my daughters, Nikki and Katie; and stepkids, Everett (and his wife, Meaghan), Annie, and Katie. My life has been deeply enriched by becoming a mom. As I reflect on my own fearless journey through the years, I can clearly see the influence our kids had on how I viewed the world. I learned from them, had my own views changed and expanded because of them, and have witnessed firsthand the potential power of this generation to change the world. Being a mom has been among the greatest privileges of my life, and I am grateful for each day with the family I love. My daughters have a loving, supportive father, Dan Villanueva, and I am grateful for the important role he has played in their lives.

When I made the decision to write this book, I turned to our treasured colleague and Case Foundation board member (and friend) Ron Klain, whose own life could be a book, having served as chief of staff to not one but two former US vice presidents. Ron knew our work with the Be Fearless principles well through the years and provided valuable insights that helped make the book possible. As a starting point, Ron fearlessly encouraged me to pursue Bob Barnett as my book agent. Bob is renowned in the publishing industry, and most especially in Washington, DC, where he has been the agent for former presidents and other luminaries. Bob's guiding hand has played a role in countless bestsellers through the years. I am enormously grateful to him for accepting this book from a first-time author and for the encouragement, wisdom, fun, and valuable expertise he brought each step of the way.

It was Bob Barnett who suggested I consider working with a collaborator and arranged for me to meet another proven veteran of the publishing industry (and of bestsellers), Catherine Whitney. Bob knew I was quite passionate about the stories I had written to convey the Be Fearless principles, and he wisely suggested that Catherine could be a valuable voice and careful eye to help shape the manuscript. The moment I met Catherine, I felt that fate was playing a role. From our very first meeting, it was clear that she shared a passion for the larger calling of this book, and for the stories we were highlighting. But it was Catherine's skilled hand that took these stories and edited, tweaked, culled, and worked with me to determine the final placements and organization of them in the book. Throughout this process, my respect and true affection for Catherine grew even stronger. I feel so fortunate to have had such a world-class collaborator, and I suspect (and hope) she will become a friend for life.

Turning this book into a reality could not have been done without the stalwart team at Simon & Schuster, all of who supported this project from the outset. In particular, I greatly appreciate the guidance and insights provided by Jonathan Karp and Richard Rhorer and the dynamic duo of Priscilla Painton and Megan Hogan, who provided careful guidance and helped to ensure the book stayed on track.

I will forever be grateful to Dr. Jane Goodall for writing the foreword to this book. Jane is an extraordinary model of fearlessness and was from such a young age. Her story reminds us that sometimes the lack of training or education can be an advantage when we set out to pursue our Big Bets. I have been deeply inspired by Jane's lifelong pursuits of justice and fairness for animals and for human beings. Few people have made such a mark, and I have been grateful that my role with the National Geographic Society has enabled my connection to her.

The intellectual property of the Be Fearless principles belongs to the Case Foundation, not to me personally, and rightfully so. I could not have written this book without the help and support of our entire team, ranging from the most senior executives right down to college interns—together as a team we researched, debated, and celebrated each aspect of the book as it came together. This is not a book by committee, but rather a thoughtful presentation of what we collectively believed would be the best way to convey the important message of the principles through storytelling. There are two individuals who should be called out for their extraordinary help and support in this process—Sam Heitner and Louise Storm. Both embraced this process as if it were their own book, providing valuable insights and reviews and keeping me focused and motivated throughout the process. I am also grateful for the contributions of Sarah Koch, who, like me, brought many years of experience at the Case Foundation teaching and sharing these principles, with an astute awareness of what often resonates in conveying them. She guided much of the research underlying the stories (together with our intern Will Potts). Jess Zetzman, who brought her marketing and social media savvy, and Jade Floyd, whose commitment over the past six years has been unwavering, brought an important eye to all the avenues we contemplated in curating the book's content. I can't do what I do at the Case Foundation without the steady, guiding hand of Brian Sasscer, a longtime valued senior executive at the Case Foundation, and someone who worked with me dating back to my AOL days. Brian, together with former Case Foundation colleagues Michael Smith, Allie Burns, and Erich Broksas, comprised the original executive team that worked with me six years ago to first bring the Be Fearless principles to life—in a sense they were cofounders of this work with me, and each provided valuable insights on the manuscript of the book as it was being finalized. I'm also grateful to our Case Foundation board for their enthusiastic support of this work over the last six years: Sean Greene, Doug Holladay, Donna Hoyle, Ron Klain, Song Pak, John Sabin, Sonal Shah, and Steve.

In addition to the Case Foundation team, we had the expertise of three important contributors to the Be Fearless work. Raphael Bemporad of BBMG, who when studying our own work at the Case Foundation came up with the title and overarching framework of Be Fearless. We then engaged the research of Brad Rourke and Cynthia Gibson, PhD, to ask a simple question: What are the common elements where transformational breakthroughs have taken place across sectors and across time? In pursuit of data to answer this question, they discovered the five principles we highlight in this book. We are grateful for these important contributions to our work that set Be Fearless on a strong path right from the start.

When we first launched Be Fearless, we invited a cross section of leaders to come be part of that special day at the Case Foundation. Our deepest thanks to Walter Isaacson, Senator Mark Warner, Tom Tierney, and Barbara Bush—daughter of former President George W. and Laura Bush—who share some credit for the remarkable embrace this work had right out of the gate. At our launch event we had hundreds of partners join us via webcast who then went on to help share the principles throughout their own organizations and with their networks, and we remain enormously grateful that many remain actively engaged with the work and enthusiastic. The same spirit can be seen six years later in the guidance and insights that Ross Baird, Genevieve Ryan, and Brad Feld provided as they reviewed early versions of this book and shows the importance of reaching out to those who can provide different perspectives to improve every project you start.

This book simply would not have been possible without the love and support of so many who have nurtured me, inspired me, loved me, and encouraged me. I've tried to convey the outsized role my mom, Norma Norton, and my grandparents, Ernest and Anna Baumgarten, had in my life. They were models of lives fearlessly lived, and of a commitment to something bigger than one's self. I'm grateful that my brothers, Jack and Jim, have had my back throughout my life, and for the love of my late sister, Judy. Jack and I speak nearly every day, and he remains a central source of love, support, and encouragement to me. After I sent this book out to Jack for a very early review of the manuscript, he read it within hours and called me bursting with pride and enthusiasm and valuable feedback. Additionally, I'm grateful for the Case Ohana (family), whom I've been fortunate to have in my life since marrying

Steve. We lost Steve's brother, Dan, to brain cancer in 2001. Dan was a fearless leader in his own right, whose life still serves as an inspiration. He cofounded Accelerate Brain Cancer Cure (ABC2) together with his wife, Stacey, Steve, and me with a commitment to accelerate therapies and a cure for this terrible disease in the years ahead.

I'm grateful to my close friend Jill Chandler for bringing me into her remarkable life story as an orphan from Korea. I had the privilege of knowing her wonderful adoptive parents in Michigan, who, with a family of three children of their own were compelled to fly to Seoul in the 1960s to bring back their much-cherished new member of the family. One more Korean child was added to the family a year later. Many thanks to Jill for allowing me to spotlight her story as part of this book (Chapter 23). Jill and I became friends long before I arrived at AOL or knew this extraordinary life of privilege, and she has stood by me with each passing chapter of life. Her steadfast support and special role in our family have meant the world to me.

Diane Wright has served as an inspiration to me for decades. A dear friend who is a talented lawyer by training, she has spent her more recent years tirelessly committing each day to making the world a better place through service in the nonprofit and faith-based realms, and that has served as an important inspiration to me through the years. I have cherished our early-morning hikes along a wooded path on the Potomac River in Virginia, where, as we walk and talk, we assess the fearlessness and purpose we are bringing to our own lives and we reflect on the role of faith in calling us to be in service to others.

Dawn Broksas is a cherished colleague I've worked with for

eighteen years and someone who has played an important role across various aspects of my life. Dawn is that quiet presence keeping everything together to allow me the freedom and flexibility to meet pressing priorities, travel, and stay connected with and supportive of those closest to me. Dawn and I share humble Midwest roots, and so, of course, it was incredibly valuable to receive her input on this book.

My sixth-grade teacher and lifelong dear friend (referenced earlier in the book), Carol Neal, provided an important review. The texts, the phone calls, and the careful eye she brought to the tone of the book ensured that the book spoke to everyone, from all walks. I could also count on her to check me on my memories of early years of which she was such a big part. We laughed about the irony of her reviewing my work since, in addition to having been my teacher, she was the faculty advisor to the yearbook staff when I was the editor . . . so a long history of her checking my work. Carol helped ignite my faith at an early age and modeled a life of serving others that truly inspired me.

My love of the written word and my love of history were ignited by Ruth Trippy, my high school English teacher, and Bob Beavin, my high school history teacher. They both opened up new worlds to me and gave me the confidence to fearlessly develop both my curiosity and ideas and to express them through the written word. The late Ken Wackes called me to excellence in my pursuits and modeled self-discipline, perseverance, and the importance of using my talents and skills for a higher purpose in life.

I write about Congressman E. Clay Shaw up front in this book, but his influence on my young life cannot be overstated. He was a gentleman to the core who was devoted to his wife and family, and utterly committed to a life of public service on behalf of his community and his nation. At a time when a lot of politicians weren't so noble (especially around young women), Clay was known for his personal and professional integrity. After his passing, I had the true privilege of telling the story of his important role in my life at the Fort Lauderdale Mayor's Prayer Breakfast that was held in his memory. More than one thousand people sat in the audience, having come to honor a man who was beloved by so many.

The fearless men and women of the National Geographic Society have served as a constant source of fearless inspiration. Some of the National Geographic stories I have shared in this book were bursting inside of me, just waiting to be told. I am in awe of the fearlessness I encounter each day in my work with National Geographic, from my time spent in the field with explorers and photographers to those working tirelessly at headquarters to champion them and bring science and exploration to life through the power of storytelling. I am grateful for the extraordinary boards of the National Geographic Society and National Geographic Partners, for which I have the honor of serving as chairman, for their own fearlessness and commitment to take risks, build unlikely partnerships, and make Big Bets as we strive to make the work of National Geographic more relevant than ever before. John Fahey, Gary Knell, and Mike Ulica are owed a special nod for the role they've played as leaders who have set the tone of fearlessness throughout the organization. In addition, I want to thank Emma Carrasco, Todd Georgelas, Courtney Rowe, and Todd Hermann, who had a hand in verifying many of the National Geographic–related elements in the book.

I'm grateful to the leaders at the Harvard Business School

Social Enterprise Initiative, Stanford Business School PACS, and Georgetown University Beeck Center, where I've had the privilege of serving. Specifically, I want to call out Tom Tierney, Laura Arrillaga-Andreessen, Alberto and Olga Maria Beeck, Sonal Shah, and Kim Meredith. The work with these great institutions has provided a deep well of knowledge and inspiration that we have integrated into our work at the Case Foundation in meaningful ways. Additionally, I want to offer thanks to the many universities across the United States that have welcomed the Be Fearless message into the classroom, at large speaking events, or across campuses. The drivers on the front lines of social innovation at these universities, most especially the students, keep us on our toes and constantly ensure the authenticity of this work.

In addition, I would be remiss if I didn't mention the inspiration from the other CEOs I serve with at other organizations I am affiliated with, including John Reher at the Brain Trust Accelerator Fund, Max Wallace at ABC2, Michael Singer at BrainScope, and Stewart McLaurin at the White House Historical Association.

Finally, I want to give thanks for the many fearless men and women of all ages and backgrounds whose stories are told in this book, and the many we lift up through other channels, such as our Be Fearless video series, case studies, and those highlighted at speaking events. Just like everyone else, I have moments that grip me and I question my own fearlessness. I am grateful for the countless stories of individuals and organizations who are out there every day making Big Bets, taking risks, making failure mater, reaching beyond their bubble, and letting urgency conquer fear. They are an inspiration to us all.

NOTES

PART ONE: MAKE A BIG BET

CHAPTER I: START RIGHT WHERE YOU ARE

4 *It wasn't long before* [Barbara Van Dahlen]: Jean Case, "Fearless Spotlight: Barbara Van Dahlen." www.casefoundation.org, March 30, 2016; also www.giveanhour.org.

6 *That woman was Madam C.J. Walker.* A'Lelia Bundles, *On Her Own Ground: The Life and Times of Madam C.J. Walker.* Scribner, 2001; madamcjwalker.com.

8 *In the late 1990s* [Brian Chesky and Joe Gebbia]: "How I Built This: Joe Gebbia." NPR, October 17, 2016; Leigh Gallagher, "The Education of Airbnb's Brian Chesky." *Fortune*, June 26, 2015; Catherine Clifford, "How the Cofounder of Airbnb Went from $25,000 in Credit Card Debt to Running His $30 Billion Company." CNBC, June 30, 2017.

11 *Imagine being a college student* [Rachel Sumekh]: "The Swipe Out Hunger Founder Is the Robin Hood of College Meal Plans." *LA Weekly*, May 3, 2017; Katie Lobosco, "She's on a Mission to Make America's Colleges Hunger-Free." CNN Money, June 12, 2017.

CHAPTER 2: BE AUDACIOUS

19 *I was too young to remember*: President John F. Kennedy, "Excerpt from the 'Special Message to the Congress on Urgent National Needs.'" May 21, 1961; John Geraci, "What Your Moonshot Can Learn from the Apollo Program." *Harvard Business Review*, April 4, 2017.

21 *Few modern organizations* [Astro Teller]: Derek Thompson, "Google X and the Science of Radical Creativity: How the Secretive Silicon Valley Lab Is Trying to Resurrect the Lost Art of Invention." *Atlantic*, November 13, 2017; Alexandra Wolfe, "Astro Teller, 'Captain of Moonshots': The Head of Alphabet's Research-and-Development Lab X Talks about Encouraging Creativity at Work, Embracing Failure and His Company's Latest Projects." *Wall Street Journal*, November 18, 2016.

23 *That's why when an innovator* [Elon Musk]: Ashlee Vance, *Elon Musk: Tesla, SpaceX, and the Quest for a Fantastic Future*. Ecco, 2015; Jethro Mullen, "Elon Musk Wants to Fly You Anywhere in the World in Less Than an Hour." CNN Tech, September 29, 2017; Nick Stockton, "Elon Musk Announces His Plan to Colonize Mars and Save Humanity." *Wired*, September 27, 2016.

24 *We live in a time of incredible audacity*: Greg Satell and Srdja Popovic, "How Protests Become Successful Social Movements." *Harvard Business Review*, January 27, 2017.

24 *Think of the Parkland #NeverAgain movement*: Charlotte Alter, "The School Shooting Generation Has Had Enough." *Time*, March 22, 2018; David S. Meyer, "The Parkland Teens Started Something. How Can It Become a Social Movement?" *Washington Post*, April 13, 2018.

24 *After hosting a national*: Joe Vanden Plas, "Jordyn Schara: From Teen Activist to Adult Difference-Maker." *InBusiness*, October 2015.

26 *If I told you that someone could* [Greyston Bakery]: Jesse Seaver, "Businesses with Impact: The Greyston Foundation and Their Open Hiring Policy." *Huffington Post*, December 6, 2017; "No Résumé? No Problem at This Yonkers Bakery." NPR, May 24, 2015.

26 *"If Chile can do it, you can"* [Michelle Bachelet]: Elizabeth Royte and Michel Greshko, "Chile Adds 10 Million Acres of Parkland in Historic First." nationalgeographic.com, January 29, 2018.

CHAPTER 3: BURST THROUGH ASSUMPTIONS

29 *There is a special photo* [Eunice Kennedy Shriver]: Eileen McNamara, *Eunice: The Kennedy Who Changed the World*. Simon & Schuster, 2018; Evan Thomas, "The Fierce Rebellion and Compassion of Eunice Shriver." *Washington Post*, April 13, 2018.

31 *One such athlete*: Lorettta Claiborne, "Let's Talk about Intellectual Disabilities." TEDxMidAtlantic, December 11, 2012; "Timothy Shriver's Greatest Spiritual Teacher." *SuperSoul Sunday*, Oprah Winfrey Network, November 23, 2014; "Aim High and Do Your Best." special olympics.org; lorettaclaiborne.com.

33 *Enric's inspiration for his*: blog/nationalgeographic.org/enricsala.

34 *She took a pair of scissors* [Sara Blakely]: Mary Logan Bikoff, "The Uplifter: How Spanx CEO Sara Blakely Became One of the Most Inspirational Women in Business." *Atlanta*, December 2017.

35 *David and Neil were MBA students*: Michael Fitzgerald, "For Warby Parker, Free Glasses Equals Clear Company Vision." *Entrepreneur*, February 10, 2015; Sean Tennerson, "Spotlight on Social Enterprise: Warby Parker." www.casefoundation.org, February 10, 2015; B. R. J. O'Donnell, "Warby Parker's Co-Founder on Starting a Company from Scratch." *Atlantic*, October 5, 2017.

37 *Attorney* [Bryan Stevenson]: Paul Barrett, "Bryan Stevenson's Death-Defying Acts." *NYU Law Magazine*, 2007.

37 *"There is this burden in America"*: James McWilliams, "Bryan Stevenson on What Well-Meaning White People Need to Know about Race." *Pacific Standard*, February 6, 2018.

CHAPTER 4: PEEK AROUND CORNERS

40 *Peeking around corners* [Jeff Bezos]: Brad Stone, *The Everything Store: Jeff Bezos and the Age of Amazon.* Little, Brown, 2013; Avery Hartmans, "The Fabulous Life of Amazon CEO Jeff Bezos, the Second-Richest Person in the World." *Business Insider*, May 15, 2017.

42 *One of my favorites is* [Sarah Parcak]: Emily Burnham, "Egyptologist from the Queen City Makes Waves in the Valley of the Kings." *Bangor Daily News*, October 6, 2011; Abigail Tucker, "Space Archaeologist Sarah Parcak Uses Satellites to Uncover Ancient Egyptian Ruins." *Smithsonian*, December 2016; Sarah Kaplan, "Meet Sarah Parcak, a High-Tech Indiana Jones, Who Just Won $1 Million for Tracking Down Antiquities Looters." *Washington Post*, November 12, 2015.

PART TWO: BE BOLD, TAKE RISKS

CHAPTER 6: GET UNCOMFORTABLE

54 *I was particularly inspired* [Eliza Scidmore]: Nina Strochlic, "The Woman Who Shaped National Geographic." *National Geographic*, February 2017; Jennifer Pococh, "Beyond the Cherry Trees: The Life and Times of Eliza Scidmore." nationalgeographic.com, March 27, 2012; Michael

E. Ruane, "Cherry Blossoms' Champion, Eliza Scidmore, Led a Life of Adventure." *Washington Post*, March 13, 2012.

55   *History is rich with stories* [Sir Ernest Shackleton]: Alasdair McGregor, "Endurance: A Glorious Antarctic Failure." *Australian Geographic*, January 22, 2015; "Shackleton's Voyage of Endurance." NOVA Online/pbs.org, February 2002.

CHAPTER 7: EMBRACE RISK AS R&D

61   *In the late 1700s, when smallpox* [Dr. Edward Jenner]: The Jenner Institute. www.jenner.ac.uk.

61   *Another great example* [Jane Goodall]: The Jane Goodall Institute. janegoodall.org; *Jane* [the movie]. National Geographic Studios, Public Road Productions, 2017.

63   *Jonas Salk took a big risk too*: Charlotte DeCroes Jacobs, *Jonas Salk: A Life*. Oxford University Press, 2015.

64   *In his celebrated book*: Eric Ries, *The Lean Startup: How Today's Entrepreneurs Use Continuous Innovation to Create Radically Successful Businesses*. Currency, 2011.

65   *To make this point*: "The Zappos Family Story." www.zappoinsights.com; Jay Yarow, "The Zappos Founder Just Told Us All Kinds of Crazy Stories—Here's the Surprisingly Candid Interview." *Business Insider*, November 28, 2011.

CHAPTER 8: PICK UP WHERE OTHERS LEFT OFF

67   *A few years ago I read*: Steven Johnson, *How We Got to Now: Six Innovations That Made the Modern World*. Riverhead Books, 2014.

70 *The micro-lending movement* [Jessica Jackley]: Nathan Chan, "How Kiva's Jessica Jackley Turned a Simple Idea into $1B in Microloans." *foundr*, March 22, 2018; also kiva.org.

71 *Microbusinesses aren't just creating*: Peter W. Roberts and Deonta D. Wortham, "The Macro Benefits of Microbusinesses." *Stanford Social Innovation Review*, January 16, 2018.

71 *Today, Steve is taking forward* [Rise of the Rest]: Andrew Ross Sorkin, "From Bezos to Walton, Big Investors Back Fund for 'Flyover' Startups." *New York Times*, December 4, 2017; Alex Konrad, "A Bevy of Billionaires Join Steve Case's $150 Million 'Rise of the Rest' Startup Fund." *Forbes*, December 5, 2017; also Rise of the Rest Seed Fund, www.revolution.com.

72 *For example, Justin Knopf, a young fifth-generation*: Miriam Horn, *Rancher, Farmer, Fisherman*. W. W. Norton & Co., 2017; Miriam Horn, "When Industrial-Scale Farming Is the Sustainable Path." *PBS NewsHour*, September 6, 2016; "Meet the Unsung Conservation Hero You're Overlooking." GreenBiz, August 27, 2016.

CHAPTER 9: RISK OR REGRET

77 Psychology Today *published*: Peter Gray, Ph.D., "Risky Play: Why Children Love It and Need It." *Psychology Today*, April 7, 2014.

77 *And yet, as*: Josh Linkner, *The Road to Reinvention: How to Drive Disruption and Accelerate Transformation*. Jossey-Bass, 2014.

77 *Consider the cautionary tale* [Kodak]: Chunka Mui, "How Kodak Failed." *Forbes*, January 18, 2012; Pete Pachal, "How Kodak Squandered Every Single Digital Opportunity It Had." Mashable, January 20, 2012; Jeremy Miller, "Instagram Took the Kodak Moment." www .stickybranding.com, March 29, 2016.

78 *Kodak's opposite would be* [Netflix]: Adam Richardson, "Netflix's Bold

Disruptive Innovation." *Harvard Business Review*, September 20, 2011; Adam Hartung, "Can Netflix Double-Pivot to Be a Media Game Changer?" *Forbes*, April 21, 2016; Bill Taylor, "How Coca-Cola, Netflix, and Amazon Learn from Failure." *Harvard Business Review*, November 10, 2017.

80 *Another quintessential pivot story* [Odeo]: Connor Simpson, "The Incredibly True (and Messy) Origin Story of Twitter." *Atlantic*, October 1, 2013; Nicholas Carlson, "The Real History of Twitter." *Business Insider*, April 13, 2011.

80 *Sony Pictures will long lament*: Ben Fritz, "The 'Black Panther' Movie Deal That Didn't Get Made." *Wall Street Journal*, February 15, 2018.

81 *Disney was smart enough*: Rob Haskell, "Disney CEO Bob Iger on Taking the Biggest Risk of His Career." *Vogue*, April 12, 2018.

CHAPTER 10: NOW GO, FIND THE "COURAGE ZONE"

83 *In her book*: Margie Warrell, *Stop Playing Safe: Rethink Risk, Unlock the Power of Courage, Achieve Outstanding Success*. Wrightbooks, 2013.

PART THREE: MAKE FAILURE MATTER

CHAPTER 11: CRASH AND LEARN

92 *With my heart in my throat*: Jean Case, "The Painful Acknowledgment of Coming Up Short." www.casefoundation.org/blog.

93 *It's a process*: Lucy Bernholz, "Failing Forward." *Alliance*, July 18, 2011.

94 *"The moonshot factory is a messy place"*: Astro Teller, "The Unexpected Benefit of Celebrating Failure." TED, April 14, 2016.

94 *Louis V. Gerstner Jr., who shepherded*: Louis V. Gerstner Jr., *Who Says Elephants Can't Dance? Leading a Great Enterprise through Dramatic Change*. HarperBusiness, 2002.

95 *Meg Whitman, the only woman*: Jeff Morganteen, "HP's Meg Whitman: One of My 'Big Failures' at eBay." CNBC, April 29, 2014.

CHAPTER 12: FAIL IN THE FOOTSTEPS OF GIANTS

98 *In a commencement address*: "Winfrey's Commencement Address." *Harvard Gazette*, May 30, 2013.

98 *Steven Spielberg was often lonely*: Eliza Berman, "Three of Steven Spielberg's Biggest Failures, According to Steven Spielberg." *Time*, October 5, 2017.

99 *Steve experienced his biggest failure*: Walter Isaacson, *Steve Jobs*. Simon & Schuster, 2011; Ruth Umoh, "How Overcoming the Fear of Failure Helped Steve Jobs, Tim Ferriss and Bill Gates Succeed." CNBC, August 7, 2017.

100 *Twenty years later*: Steve Jobs, "You've Got to Find What You Love." Stanford University commencement address. *Stanford News*, June 14, 2005.

100 *One of Steve's most profitable*: Maria Popova, "Pixar Cofounder Ed Catmull on Failure and Why Fostering a Fearless Culture Is the Key to Groundbreaking Creative Work." Brainpickings.

102 *Kelly Clark*: Karen Rosen, "Five-Time Olympian Kelly Clark Looks Back on Her Career and Influencing the Next Generation of Snowboarders." www.teamusa.org, February 14, 2018; Jean Case, "What to Look for During the Olympics." www.casefoundation.org/blog, February 5, 2018.

102 *Richard Branson's failures*: Alp Mimaroglu, "What Richard Branson Learned from His Seven Biggest Failures." *Entrepreneur*, July 18, 2017.

CHAPTER 13: BEAT THE ODDS

105   *At her lowest*: J. K. Rowling, "The Fringe Benefits of Failure, and the Importance of Imagination." Harvard University commencement address. *Harvard Gazette*, June 5, 2008.

106   *In 2016, Rowling posted*: Anjelica Oswald, "Even Rockstar Author J. K. Rowling Has Received Letters of Rejection." *Business Insider*, July 29, 2016.

106   *When eleven-year-old Salva Dut's village*: Linda Sue Park, *A Long Walk to Water: Based on a True Story*. Clarion Books, 2010; Salva Dut, "I Kept Walking." TEDxYouth@Beacon St., December 21, 2016; also waterforsudan.org.

108   *"You have an eighteen-year-old boy"*: Jake Wood, "A New Mission for Veterans—Disaster Relief." TEDxSanDiego, December 2011; also https//teamrubiconusa.org.

109   *"I embrace my past"* [Darren Walker]: Jonathan Capehart, "Darren Walker: Using Privilege to Fight Privilege." *Washington Post*, August 30, 2016.

CHAPTER 14: TAKE THE LONG VIEW

112   *The Gates Foundation announced*: Bill and Melinda Gates Foundation, www.gatesfoundation.org.

114   *In the midst of the celebration*: Adam Kilgore, " 'It's Never Easy,' but Ted Leonsis Delivered D.C. a Title and a Team to Take Pride In." *Washington Post*, June 10, 2018.

114   *Before you label someone* [Milton S. Hershey]: Hershey Community Archives, hersheyarchives.org.

116   *"On the road to great achievement"*: Malcolm Gladwell, "Late Bloomers: Why Do We Equate Genius with Precocity?" *New Yorker*, October 20, 2008.

116 *Warren Buffett is an extraordinarily successful*: https://buffett.cnbc.com /video/2018/03/25/buffett-on-the-dumbest-stock-I-ever-bought.html.

PART FOUR: REACH BEYOND YOUR BUBBLE

CHAPTER 16: ELIMINATE BLIND SPOTS

128 *In 2017, my friend*: Ross Baird, *The Innovation Blind Spot: Why We Back the Wrong Ideas—and What to Do About It*. BenBella Books, 2017.

129 *His book seems in many respects*: Adam Grant, *Originals: How Non-Conformists Move the World*. Viking, 2016; Steve Case, *The Third Wave: An Entrepreneur's Vision of the Future*. Simon & Schuster, 2016.

129 *The former steel town*: Jean Case, "Getting in the Arena: Good Ideas and Innovations Often Come from Unexpected Places." www.case foundation.org/blog, April 27, 2017.

130 *Pittsburgh innovator range*: Note that Jean and Steve Case are investors in SolePower.

CHAPTER 17: BUILD UNLIKELY PARTNERSHIPS

133 *And research supports this*: Vivian Hunt, Dennis Layton, and Sara Prince, *Diversity Matters*. McKinsey & Company, February 2, 2015, https://assets.mckinsey.com/~/media/857F440109AA4D13A54D9C 496D86ED58.ashx.

135 *This same enterprise model*: Laura Parker, "National Geographic and 21st Century Fox Expand Media Partnership." nationalgeographic .com, September 9, 2015.

136 *Consider the unlikely partnership* [NASA/LEGO]: Matt Blum, "Lego and NASA Build a Partnership for Education." *Wired*, November 14, 2014.

136 *Earlier I described* [Airbnb/KLM]: Ben Mutzabaugh, "KLM MD-11 Listed as 'Spacious Airline Apartment' on Airbnb." *USA Today*, November 14, 2014.

137 *Another great example* [impact investing]: Paul Sullivan, "How to Invest with a Conscience (and Still Make Money)." *New York Times*, March 16, 2018; Elizabeth MacBride, "Jean Case Calls On Wall Street to Embrace Impact Investing." cnbc.com, May 17, 2018; Ryan Derousseau, "How Impact Investing Can Put a Profitable Spin on Charity." *Fortune*, December 13, 2017; Jean Case, "New Year's Resolution: Invest with an Eye on Impact." www.casefoundation.org/blog, December 27, 2017; Jean Case, "Bringing the Last Decade of Impact Investing to Life: An Interactive Timeline." www.casefoundation.org/blog, November 17, 2017.

138 *One of my favorite examples* [Jill Andrews]: Jessica Contrera, "How the Fight against Ebola Came to New York Fashion Week." *Washington Post*, February 15, 2015; Anne Quito, "A Wedding Gown Designer Gave the Ebola Hazmat Suit a Makeover." *Quartz*, February 19, 2015.

139 *Melinda Gates affirmed this*: "What Nonprofits Can Learn from Coca-Cola." TED, September 2010.

140 *One of the most meaningful*: Harold Varmus, "Making PEPFAR: A Triumph of Medical Diplomacy." *Science & Diplomacy*, December 1, 2013; Myra Sessions, "Overview of the President's Emergency Plan for AIDS Relief (PEPFAR)." Center for Global Development, https://www.cgdev.org/page/overview-president%E2%80%99s-emergency-plan-aids-relief-pepfar.

142 *In an interview, Bono*: Sheryl Gay Stolberg, "The World: A Calling to Heal; Getting Religion on AIDS." *New York Times*, February 2, 2003.

CHAPTER 18: BE BETTER TOGETHER

146 *I love Lin-Manuel Miranda's* Hamilton: Spencer Kornhaber, "Hamilton: Casting After Colorblindness." *Atlantic*, March 31, 2016; Rob Weinert-Kendt, "Rapping a Revolution." *New York Times*, February 5, 2015.

147 *In creating* Hamilton: Ron Chernow, *Alexander Hamilton*. Penguin Press, 2004.

147 *When they expanded*: Vivian Hunt, Sara Prince, Sundiatu Dixon-Fyle, and Lareina Yee, *Delivering Through Diversity*. McKinsey & Company, January 2018, https://www.mckinsey.com/~/media/mckinsey /business%20functions/organization/our%20insights/delivering%20 through%20diversity/delivering-through-diversity_full-report.ashx.

147 *When Deloitte reported*: Juliet Bourke, Stacia Garr, Addie van Berkel, Jungle Wong, "Diversity and Inclusion: The Reality Gap." Deloitte Insights, February 28, 2017.

148 *And in 2018,* Forbes *published*: Jeff Kauflin, "America's Best Employers for Diversity." *Forbes*, January 23, 2018.

148 *The numbers are stark*: Pat Wechsler, "Women-Led Companies Perform Three Times Better Than the S&P 500." *Fortune*, March 3, 2015; Jena McGregor, "Why It's Smart to Invest in Women-Led Companies." *Washington Post*, August 2, 2017.

151 *She tells a story*: Mellody Hobson, "Color Blind or Color Brave?" TED, March 2014.

151 *The great conductor*: Claudia Goldin and Cecilia Rouse, "Orchestrating Impartiality: The Impact of 'Blind' Auditions on Female Musicians." National Bureau of Economic Research, January 1997.

152 *When I came across the story*: Dame Stephanie Shirley, "Why Do Ambitious Women Have Flat Heads?" TED, March 2015.

153 *Another one of my favorite* [Vernice Armour]: "Black Female Pilot Breaks Racial, Gender Barriers." NPR, May 27, 2011.

154   *In 2016, I was invited* [Barbara Hackman Franklin]: Jean Case, "One Fearless Question That Paved the Way for Women in Government." www.casefoundation.org/blog, March 8, 2016.

CHAPTER 19: LEVERAGE PARTNERSHIPS FOR GROWTH

161   *Take a lesson from Liberia* [Last Mile Health]: Claudia Dreifus, "Dr. Raj Panjabi Goes the Last Mile in Liberia." *New York Times*, July 31, 2017.

162   *John Doerr, in telling the story*: John Doerr, *Measure What Matters: How Google, Bono, and the Gates Foundation Rock the World with OKRs.* Portfolio, 2018.

163   *In late 2004, after an earthquake*: Bob Woodruff, "People of the Year: Bill Clinton and George H. W. Bush." *ABC World News Tonight*, December 27, 2005.

CHAPTER 20: NOW GO, GET OUTSIDE YOUR BUBBLE ... EVERY DAY

165   *And as Stephen R. Covey recommends*: Stephen R. Covey, *The 7 Habits of Highly Effective People: Powerful Lessons in Personal Change.* Simon & Schuster, 2013.

PART FIVE: LET URGENCY CONQUER FEAR

CHAPTER 21: SEIZE THE MOMENT

170   *One of the iconic stories*: Jennifer Latson, "How Poisoned Tylenol Became a Crisis-Management Teaching Model." time.com, September

29, 2014; Judith Rehak, "Tylenol Made a Hero of Johnson & Johnson." *International Herald Tribune*, March 23, 2002.

171 *In his book*: Steve Case, *The Third Wave: An Entrepreneur's Vision of the Future*. Simon & Schuster, 2016.

173 *Corrie ten Boom was an unmarried*: Corrie ten Boom, *The Hiding Place: The Triumphant Story of Corrie ten Boom*. Barbour Books, 2000; www.corrietenboom.com.

CHAPTER 22: BE A FIRST RESPONDER

177 *Walmart has often been criticized*: Michael Barbaro and Justin Gillis, "Wal-Mart at Forefront of Hurricane Relief." *Washington Post*, September 6, 2005.

178 *After the storm*: Lee Scott, "Twenty First Century Leadership." corporate.walmart.com, October 23, 2005.

179 *José Andrés calls himself*: Maura Judkis, "José Andrés on the Moment That Changed the Way He Thought about Charity." *Washington Post*, March 12, 2018; Jean Case, "Finding Light in the Darkness." www.casefoundation.org/blog, January 10, 2018.

182 *Paul Rieckhoff never planned*: Paul Rieckhoff, *Chasing Ghosts: Failure and Façades in Iraq: A Soldier's Perspective*. NAL Hardcover, 2006.

CHAPTER 23: DON'T OVERTHINK OR OVERANALYZE. DO.

185 *In her book*: Mel Robbins, *The 5 Second Rule: Transform Your Life, Work, and Confidence with Everyday Courage*. Savio Republic, 2017.

186 *In their book*: Ryan Babineaux and John Krumboltz, *Fail Fast, Fail Often: How Losing Can Help You Win*. TarcherPerigee, 2013.

187   *But as Geithner notes*: Timothy F. Geithner, *Stress Test: Reflections on Financial Crises*. Crown, 2014.

187   *President Obama announced*: My Brother's Keeper [MBK] Alliance. The Obama Foundation, obama.org/mbka/.

188   *In 1954, Bertha and Harry Holt*: Holt International, holtinternational.org.

190   *Marta Gabre-Tsadick has spent*: Project Mercy/Marta's Story. www .projectmercy.org; Marta Gabre-Tsadick, *Sheltered by the King*. Chosen Books, 1983.

193   *"It is not the critic who counts"*: Theodore Roosevelt, "Citizenship in a Republic." Speech delivered at the Sorbonne in Paris, France, April 23, 1910, http:// www.theodore-roosevelt.com/images/research/speeches/maninthearena.pdf.

194   *Noted professor, author, and speaker*: Brené Brown, *Daring Greatly: How the Courage to Be Vulnerable Transforms the Way We Live, Love, Parent, and Lead*. Avery, 2012.

CHAPTER 24: NOW GO, BE THE ONE

195   *"We are what we choose"*: "Remarks by Jeff Bezos, as Delivered to the Class of 2010, Baccalaureate." Princeton University, May 30, 2010.

196   *In his book*: Tom Peters, *The Excellence Dividend: Meeting the Tech Tide with Work That Wows and Jobs That Last*. Vintage, 2018.

196   *As John Kotter of Harvard Business School*: Paul Michelman with John Kotter, "The Importance of Urgency." Harvard Business Ideacast, August 2008.

INDEX

ABOUT THE AUTHOR

Jean Case, the first female Chairman of the National Geographic Society in its 130-year history and CEO of the Case Foundation, is a philanthropist, investor, and Internet and impact-investing pioneer who advocates for the importance of embracing a more fearless approach to innovate and bring about transformational breakthroughs. Her career in the private sector spanned nearly two decades before she cofounded the Case Foundation in 1997.

Before the Case Foundation, she was a senior executive at America Online, Inc., where she directed the marketing and branding as AOL brought the Internet to the masses.

In addition, Jean currently serves on the boards of Accelerate Brain Cancer Cure (ABC2), the White House Historical Association, and BrainScope Company, Inc., as well as on the advisory boards of the Brain Trust Accelerator Fund, the Stanford Center on Philanthropy and Civil Society, and Georgetown University's Beeck Center for Social Impact & Innovation. She was elected to the American Academy of Arts & Sciences in 2016 and has received honorary degrees from Indiana University and George Mason University. *Be Fearless: 5 Principles for a Life of Breakthroughs and Purpose* is her first book.